D1012911

MUGGED BY A MOOSE

True Tales to make you Laugh, Chortle,
Snicker and Feel Inspired

WATCH OUT FOR THOSE, Moose!

Matt Jackson

Edited by Matt Jackson
Summit Studios

Copyright © 2006 by Summit Studios. All rights reserved.
Introduction copyright © 2006 by Matthew Jackson

The use of any part of this publication reproduced, transmitted in any form or by any means, electronic, mechanical, photocopying, recording, or otherwise, or stored in a retrieval system, without the prior written consent of the publisher—or, in case of photocopying or other reprographic copying, a license from the Canadian Copyright Licensing Agency—is an infringement of copyright law.

Library and Archives Canada Cataloguing in Publication

Mugged by a moose : true tales to make you laugh, chortle, snicker and feel inspired / edited by Matt Jackson. -- Canadian ed.

ISBN 0-9734671-3-4
    1. Outdoor life--Humor. I. Jackson, Matt
PN6178.C3M84 2006   796.5'0971   C2006-902511-8

Designed by Kirk Seton, Signet Design Solutions
Cover photograph by Robert McCaw
Printed and Bound in Canada

SUMMIT STUDIOS
#105-2572 Birch St.
Vancouver, British Columbia
V6H 2T4 Canada

This book is dedicated to all of those who venture bravely into the great outdoors and come back with stories to share.

Table of Contents

Introduction

By Matt Jackson

A university acquaintance once told me a story about a canoe trip he took in Ontario's Algonquin Provincial Park, one of the province's oldest and most cherished wilderness parks. With more than 7,500 square kilometres of boreal forest and hundreds of bogs, lakes, and rivers, Algonquin is an ideal playground for canoeists. It is also an ideal home for moose, so it's not surprising that people travel from all over the world to see these animals in their natural habitat.

Several days into the trip my acquaintance and his paddling partner finally got their chance. They rounded the corner on a long portage and spotted a bull moose grazing on some aquatic plants about a hundred metres from the trail. They dropped their packs and whispered excitedly to one another. This was the moment they had been waiting for.

After a few moments the moose looked up and stared at them. For whatever reason, he decided he wasn't happy about having his meal disturbed. He snorted loudly, bellowed, and charged through the forest toward the startled canoeists, his antlers thrashing wildly through the underbrush.

My acquaintance told me he's never been able to dunk a basketball, and yet he managed to leap more than ten feet to reach the nearest tree branch. There, he and his friend sat for "a very long time," while the angry moose paced around the base, snorting and stomping his hooves.

I wasn't sure what to think of this yarn when I first heard it. Had the canoeists been taunting the moose? Had they flashed their red underwear at him? Was the story even true? I was a bit skeptical. Since then, I've heard several anecdotes and had personal encounters with moose that have convinced me it's probably true.

It would be downright unfair, of course, to paint moose as nothing more than big outdoor bullies. Yet there's no question they can be ornery and temperamental at times. Any seasoned outdoorsperson knows that you don't want to cross paths with a bull protecting his territory during the fall rut. Or a cow protecting her calf in the spring.

Some of the moose encounters I've heard about are absolutely unbelievable. They've not only inspired the title for this collection of true tales, they've inspired the story with the same name, which I will let you read for yourself without giving away any juicy tidbits. Let's just say you haven't really experienced a bad day on the road until you've had a moose jump off a roadside cliff and land on your red sports car.

Compiling this book has been a real pleasure, and I've selected stories for a variety of reasons. I've always preferred books that keep readers on their toes, which is why I've resisted the temptation to lump stories into neat little categories. Besides, a story that makes one reader laugh uncontrollably might fall flat with another. Likewise, a story that inspires some readers might mean nothing to somebody else. Still, many of these tales will hopefully coax some laughs, chortles, snickers, and giggles from you, as writers share some of the laughable predicaments they've found themselves in.

A few of these situations are self-perpetuated, such as when Brent Curry builds something resembling a two-person bicycle using his living room couch, and then talks his unsuspecting Danish friend into joining him on a "bike" trip the length of Prince Edward Island. As Curry relates in his story, he figured that because English was his friend's second language, he wouldn't readily question the odd juxtaposition of phrases like "ninety-five-pound chesterfield" with "self-contained bicycle travel."

Other situations took our contributors completely by surprise, such as when Terry Gowler watched with horror as his wedding ring slipped from his finger and fell into Barkley Sound on a sea kayaking trip. Another of my favourites, which is more apt to create a general sense of awe or wonderment, is about Hazel Booth and three friends who rescued a moose from drowning in an icy Yukon lake.

There are even a couple of epic adventures that you won't want to "try at home," but are nevertheless great to read about. Join Marty McLennan for the first-ever traverse of Russia's Kamchatka Peninsula on a bicycle, riding on roads as greasy as a cookie sheet. Another story features two accidental adventurers from Britain who initially wanted nothing more than a summer canoe vacation in Canada. Three years later they arrived at the mouth of the Amazon River in Brazil, having survived frostbite on the Mississippi, dodged bullets in Nicaragua, and portaged five hundred pounds of gear across a seventy-five-kilometre desert in northern Columbia. And to think they funded their trip by selling hats made out of palm fronds.

We all venture into the outdoors for different reasons. Some of us go to challenge ourselves, to purposely put an element of hardship into our lives that modern technology and comforts have largely eradicated. Some seek escape from the workday hustle and bustle, finding solace in something as simple as the rhythm of a paddle stroke, or the smell of morning coffee brewing on a campfire.

Yet others go for the Great Unknown, the simple mystery of not knowing what lies around the next bend in the river, or over the next mountain ridge. It might be a crimson sun setting the clouds on fire, sinking slowly into the Pacific. Or a summer shower that will bring out the sweet scent of a pine forest. Or a pocket of blueberry bushes ripe for harvest.

Then again, it might be the sound of an angry moose charging through the forest toward you, right after you've dropped your drawers to relieve yourself. Maybe next time you'll leave your red underwear at home.

Predatory Rites

Finding one's place in the Polar food chain.

By Philip Torrens

There is nothing quite like the experience of nearly being eaten to make you appreciate how fleeting your position atop the food chain is. In the summer of 1993, I became one of the lucky few to acquire this sort of insight.

Backcountry tourists, as opposed to those who live in the wilderness, seem to fall into two equally simple-minded groups. Those of the old school are convinced that behind every bush, a predator lurks expressly for them. They are barely able to stagger down trails under the burden of rifles and grenade launchers. Late-night forays to answer the call of nature are made perilous by the razor wire and minefields they have used to "secure" the camp perimeter. These folks have delusions about their own importance in the scheme of things.

Equally naive in their own sweet way, members of the other school skip down trails strung out on alfalfa sprouts, certain that the woodland critters will sense the purity and goodwill bursting from their little whole-wheat hearts and love them for it. The beasties will love them, all right—for their nutritional content.

You may be attacked if you happen to fit a creature's dietary needs, or if you appear to be threatening its young. Try not to take it personally—that's just life in the wild. With the same lack of malice, forced to choose, I would rather kill than be killed. (I believe as much as anyone that predators are among nature's most marvellous creations. I also believe the perfection of their bodies is best appreciated from the outside.) With this in mind, my travel partner Mark and I carried a shotgun on our trip from Inuvik down the Mackenzie River to the Beaufort Sea.

The federal government publishes an earnest and unintentionally hilarious pamphlet on bear attacks. To respond correctly to an encounter, it solemnly counsels, first determine what species of bear you are confronted with. If it's a black bear, do not bother climbing a tree, as it will bound up after you. Grizzlies, on the other paw, supposedly do not climb trees well. This is reassuring until you learn that a grizzly may weigh up to 600 kilograms. Any tree he cannot readily knock over, he can probably shake you from as though harvesting a ripe apple.

In any case, how does one tell the difference between species? It's easy—simply take a good, close look at the claws. If they're hooked, it's a probably a black bear; if they're gently arched, it's a grizz that's got you…

Given that we were travelling above the Arctic Circle, neither black bears nor trees seemed likely encounters, so we acquired a second booklet from the government of the Northwest Territories. It was full of sensible advice, with one discouraging exception regarding polar bears.

Polar bears live in the North, and are a vital part of the traditional lifestyle. Guided bear hunting—and the subsequent skinning of both bears and Southern hunters—adds thousands of badly needed dollars to the economies of northern hamlets. Due to their larger breeding populations, tourists are far more easily replaced than bears, and the Hunters' and Trappers' Cooperatives do not want bears killed frivolously. The brochure therefore requests that you not shoot at a bear unless it comes within ten metres.

We are talking about an animal that can move faster than a racehorse, with a skull that is armoured like a tank. I confess that we decided we would open fire at any bear within shotgun range and re-erect the tent within ten metres of any resulting casualties.

After kayaking down the Mackenzie River and along the edge of the Beaufort Sea, we arrived at a point about three hundred kilometres northeast of the teeming (with mosquitoes) hamlet of Tuktoyaktuk.

"Our" bear cunningly waited until we both lay asleep in our cozy tent at five o'clock one morning. My first hint of trouble was a violent cuff to my forehead, which spun me from my back onto my stomach. This was followed by a low growl in my ear and claws driven deep into my right shoulder. I reacted instinctively, mumbling something vague about being too tired and having to work in the morning, and curled tightly into a fetal position. When the unwelcome attentions persisted, I came to suspect that something was amiss. Strengthened in this conviction by the sight of the tent wall being hit—apparently by a battering ram, to the tune of hearty baritone bellows—I hastily quit my bed. Or rather, tried to.

For a realistic simulation of what it is like to extricate yourself from a mummy sleeping bag in such circumstances, you may want to have a friend dump you into a burlap sack, secure the drawstring with a granny knot, and wallop you with a baseball bat at random but frequent intervals while you try to get out. Then again, you may very well not want to do so. There's no accounting for taste.

Mark, who had initially attributed the thumps and cries from my side of the tent to a nightmare on my part (which, in a sense, was correct), now sat up and rapidly revised his assessment: "A bear! It's a bear!"

I had become convinced of this on my own, but it was reassuring to have him concur. I could be satisfied that I was not advocating hastily opening fire on what might only turn out to be a socially disadvantaged ground squirrel whose crack cocaine habit was a desperate cry for help.

The motion to shoot having been quickly debated, seconded, and passed, the only remaining logistical difficulty was locating the shotgun. It was buried beneath the fallen nylon fabric and aluminum poles, which were (unaccountably) failing to withstand the assault.

Compounding the problem, the bear—as is typical of all large, hairy bullies—refused to allow a time out for me to locate my glasses. In the end, I was forced to kick at the collapsed side of the tent in an effort to dig up the gun. Just as I succeeded and tossed the weapon to Mark, the bear seized my foot in its mouth. I spent an exhilarating few seconds being whipped back and forth on the end of my leg. I recommend the experience to anyone who's ever wondered what it feels like to be the mouse the cat plays with.

The next item on the bear's agenda seemed to be either to chew off my size nine-and-a-half foot as an appetizer or to drag me from the tent, where it would be easier to fillet me into McNuggets. Fortunately, my coolly improvised, two-tiered counterattack—which combined my overripe socks with eardrum-piercing shrieks—forced the bear to gag momentarily. I quickly pulled my leg out of range.

Mark had the gun ready by now, but prudently remembered that a non-lethal hit on a bear merely worsens its disposition. We could not see our attacker through the tent, so he fired a warning round at the roof, which he managed to hit with his very first shot.

Since I was momentarily indisposed, Mark was left with the unenviable task of sticking his head out through the top of the tent, not knowing if he was going to have his noggin knocked off for his trouble. Fortunately, Brother Bear had beat feet outta there.

In hindsight, the reason for the attack was almost certainly the food odour on our tent. I can hear the righteous wails arising from across the nation. *Everybody* knows you don't eat in or near your tent in bear country. Everybody, Mark and I included, *does* know that.

However, even in the summer, a heat-leeching wind steals almost continually across the Arctic. The only sure way to rekindle the body's inner fires after long, cold hours at sea in a kayak is by consuming hot food. And the only way to keep food hot long enough to do any good is to keep it out of the wind. And the only place out of the wind above the treeline is … in your tent. So call it a (badly) miscalculated risk.

One ironic aspect of all this one-sided shadow boxing is that we never actually saw our assailant well enough to figure out what sort of bear it was. Since that same inability to see undoubtedly prevented the bear from killing me, I won't complain.

During the subsequent investigation, the Wildlife Department biologist expressed the opinion, based on the location and time of year, that it was probably a polar bear. If so, I am even luckier than I had imagined, as polar bears are one of the few animals that actively hunt humans.

Overall, we got off extraordinarily lightly. We did not have to kill one of nature's noblest creations (thank Heaven for that—the paperwork is endless if one does). I bear (sorry about that) a very faint mark on my forehead, which I feel I can legitimately pass off as a duelling scar. My right shoulder features claw marks that will require earnest and detailed explanation to any future inamorata, and the minor wound in my right foot doubles as a handy barometer. We look forward to resolving our dispute with the tent manufacturer over what constitutes non-warrantied "product abuse" any day now.

People naturally ask whether this experience has left me afraid to venture into the wilderness, or whether it has changed my backcountry habits. Certainly not. You may encounter me on a backcountry trail anytime soon. I'll be the one in the stainless steel underwear.

A Vancouver writer, Philip Torrens is a seasoned backcountry paddler—though apparently not to every bear's taste.

High Above the Rat Race

What goes up must eventually come down.

By Jason Hoerle

I deserved to take a road trip. It was October 1994 and I had just finished the end-of-season closure duties at Whitehorn Lodge, perched halfway up the Lake Louise Ski Area in Banff National Park. It had been a spectacular restaurant to manage during the summer, although the stress of staff conflicts and tourists who asked questions like, "Do y'all have laws here in Canada?" had taken their toll on me. I mean, how many daft questions can you answer before jumping off a chairlift?

The road trip, I told myself, would help to prepare me for the coming winter season, and I could think of no more appealing trip than to cruise leisurely down the west coast of Oregon and California. It was *my* turn to sit in restaurants, order food, drink wine, and ask daft questions. Indeed, it was time for a little R & R (revenge and retaliation).

I was young, energetic, single, and the proud owner of a Volkswagen Golf that ran on diesel. It had performed well since prehistoric times, and was good for at least nine hundred clicks on twenty bucks. I wanted to live a road trip dream of cheap kilometres, American burger joints, incredible ocean vistas, and tents pitched in sleepy little towns where police officers don't look beyond the rims of their steaming coffee mugs.

I started my dream journey by driving to Vancouver, then cutting south past the Seattle Space Needle. Oregon's sprawling beaches were next, followed by California's sequoias. I drove right onto Haight and Ashbury in San Francisco, and spent several days exploring the Bay area—riding its street cars, dining in bistros on Fisherman's Wharf and romping through its many green areas. I even biked across the Golden Gate Bridge.

I had just learned to rock climb and over the previous couple of years had become an avid scrambler and mountaineer. I hadn't tackled anything too difficult, but more or less enjoyed getting to the top of anything where a worthy view awaited me. It's for that reason that I detoured inland from San Francisco to Yosemite's soaring granite before continuing southeast to Mount Whitney in the Sierra Nevada Range.

For those unfamiliar with climbing, I should mention here that Mount Whitney is the highest peak in the lower continental United States. Although the mountain has a non-technical route (where climbing equipment is not necessary), its summit stands at an impressive 4,418 metres (14,494 feet) above sea level. I was certain the view would be more than worthy—and, frankly, the idea of standing above 266 million Americans running the rat race kind of appealed to me. So I registered to hike the twenty-seven round-trip kilometres to the summit and back.

It was early November by this time and low-season traffic allowed a relaxed atmosphere for hiking. I prepared for my ascent in a town called Lone Pine and relished the moment I took to the trail at Whitney Portal. The blue skies were a good omen, and I enjoyed a stiff hike up to Trail Camp, where I pitched my tent at over 3,600 metres (12,000 feet). The stars were unbelievably bright. The stress from all those hectic days running the restaurant simply evaporated into the crisp mountain air.

When I awoke the next morning, I had a very slight case of nausea. Acute Mountain Sickness (AMS) affects many people who climb above 4,000 metres (13,000 feet), so I wasn't really surprised; I had ascended very quickly. Gratefully, the feeling was easily offset by the excitement of being on such a big mountain. Feeling elated, I started hiking early and after five long hours was cresting the ridge past Mount Muir and onto Mount Whitney's summit.

A panoramic view extending hundreds of kilometres greeted me, and I was alone to enjoy it. No one else was on the summit. Bright sunshine warmed my face, despite a powerful wind that buffeted the pinnacle. I was the highest person in the Lower 48 and it felt, well ... nauseous. Still, I realized that there were millions of people living below me—driving to work, making lunch, kissing goodbye at bus stops or shopping at Wal-Mart. Maybe a few of them felt nauseous, too. After a few minutes of such contemplation, my nausea and pounding head drove me from the top.

Decreased coordination is often a side effect of moderate AMS, but as I descended I felt in control. It's true, my head was pounding and the rhythm of my steps was slightly off kilter, but it didn't seem serious. I continued to drink water, and with every step descended to a lower elevation. The temperature was starting to warm up, too.

A series of switchbacks lies just south of Mount Muir along the regular descent route. I could see my campsite nestled beside a small lake. I evaluated the switchbacks that had brought me to the summit, but my attention was drawn instead to a snow gully that appeared ripe for a glissade. A glissade is when a mountaineer descends a snow slope on his backside, using the pick of his ice axe to control his speed as he slides. It can be thrilling. I was feeling much better by this time and realized that glissading down would also get me into town that much sooner for a well-earned cheeseburger and Budweiser.

Glissades are especially enjoyable when snow conditions are right and the pitch is not too steep. I gripped my ice axe firmly and started to descend, checking my speed. The sun had softened the snow slope and it was sheer enjoyment. A little lower, however, the soft snow developed a firmer constitution. I crested a headwall and before I realized it, the pitch had steepened significantly. Engulfed in shade, the snow was now a sheet of ice on a forty-five-degree slope, and my glissade speed increased dramatically. Panicking a bit, I pressed harder with the pick of my axe, but it could no longer penetrate the surface ice.

Then there came a worrisome sound: the sharp *ping!* of my ice axe hitting a rock and being ripped from my grasp. And yet another noise, like a zipper being yanked open. It was the sound of my Gore-Tex clothing against the ice face as I careened down the mountain at terminal velocity. It was a high-pitched whizzing sound that, I'm certain, matched my heart rate beat for beat. I felt as helpless as a turtle hurtling down a luge run on its backside.

That's when I noticed the massive boulders below me, yawning like giant teeth. It was a moment of sheer terror: you know, one of those moments when time is suspended just long enough for you to assess the situation, even though you have absolutely no control over the outcome. "Why didn't you take the switchbacks?" was all I could think. Maybe serving tea to busloads of tourists was a noble occupation; it's certainly much safer.

A moment later, I felt a jolt, and a searing pain shot through my arm. I was airborne. For a split second, the sound of a rapidly opening zipper ceased. Then I slammed hard against the ice, breaking its hard shell. Ice crystals exploded, covering my face, even as snow filled all the nooks and crannies of my clothing.

I had stopped! I was alive!

I lay there, trying to catch my breath, exulting in my intactness, my oneness with nature. My heart was still racing, and my arm began to throb. Eventually I looked up to see what had stopped my descent. Apparently I had clipped a protruding rock with my arm while spinning down the gully, and the impact had lifted my body off the ice. I landed with just enough force to break through the crust—less than forty metres from the boulder garden at the bottom of the gully.

Shaking and humbled, I retrieved my tent and made quick time back to Lone Pine, following those beautiful switchbacks the entire way. I left my ice axe on the mountain, an offering that will hopefully protect the next daft hiker who has overly ambitious glissade fantasies.

Jason Hoerle lives with his wife Lindsey and daughter Beatrice in Canmore, Alberta, where he hikes, bikes, skis and climbs whenever possible. He's recently produced a line of mountain sculptures that can be viewed at www.altiplanodesigns.ca.

Mugged by a Moose

Hand over your wallet and jewellery … and you may as well give me that golf cart while you're at it.

By Matt Jackson

Moose are on the loose in Ontario's Algonquin Provincial Park, and they have been known to mug canoeists from time to time. Just ask Craig Keates, who recently spent five days paddling through the southern part of the park.

It was a drizzly Friday evening when Craig and his girlfriend heard a loud chomping noise a few metres from their campsite. When they trained a flashlight beam in the direction of the sound, it revealed a pair of glowing eyes in the forest. Unable to determine what kind of animal it was—and reluctant to hang around and find out—the pair retreated down a steep embankment to the relative safety of their canoe.

Several long minutes passed. The couple was getting cold and wet, so they eventually decided to climb back up the embankment, build up the fire, bang some pots and pans together, and gather a few items in case they had to retreat again. At the top of the bank, they suddenly came face to snout with their late-night visitor: a massive moose standing at the edge of their campsite, staring right at them.

The moose seemed passive, and it soon returned to eating, so Craig and his girlfriend decided to try sharing the campsite with the animal. They settled themselves by the firepit and carried on as normal.

Over the next ten or fifteen minutes, the moose continued feeding, but in a direction that brought it closer and closer to them. Before long, it was standing three or four metres away from the firepit, and the campers were starting to feel a little anxious.

As Craig tells it, he muttered "a few choice words" at the animal, which prompted the moose to stop eating, turn, stare at the couple, and then start walking toward them with "greater purpose" than it had displayed thus far.

That was enough. Craig and his girlfriend beat a hasty retreat down the embankment, and when they looked up the cliff face from the bottom, they could see the moose peering over the edge at them from above.

Reluctantly, they climbed into their canoe and pushed off from shore. As they paddled away from the campsite into the cold and drizzly night, they were treated to a very bizarre sight: the moose was standing directly in front of the firepit, warming itself.

As for Craig and his girlfriend, they spent a wet night partially shielded from the rain by a crude lean-to shelter they fashioned out of their canoe and some pine boughs.

*   *   *

Most Canadians think of the moose as a large, dopey animal that was basically assembled using all of God's spare parts. Consider the odd combination of stubby tail, gangly legs, droopy snout, and the strange dewlap of skin that hangs from a moose's neck; all these pieces make them look rather preposterous. Add to this the moose's vacant stare and typically ponderous manner, and you have what appears to be a bumbling Bullwinkle.

There's more to a moose than its outward appearance, of course. Moose may be somewhat clumsy looking, but I doubt most Canadians realize that a muscular bull can weigh as much as 725 kilograms (or 1,600 pounds) and can stand 2.1 metres (that's seven feet) tall at the shoulders. You may also be unaware that a motivated moose can run fifty-six kilometres per hour, or dive up to six metres under the water to search for aquatic plants.

Furthermore, you probably don't know that your average moose is also quite capable of chasing a terrified wildlife biologist off the end of a peninsula, up a leaning pine, and into a moving boat. This very thing happened to wildlife researcher Dale Garner in Algonquin Park when he got too close to a mother moose and her calf.

"In hindsight, the timing was perfect," says Gardner, "considering the boat was moving when I jumped from the tree."

Yes, it's fair to say that moose can be belligerent, fearless, and more than a little unpredictable. There are accounts of moose charging at oncoming locomotives and departing planes. So if you happen to spot one grazing placidly in the wild, just remember that the next moment it might be bellowing and charging through the forest at you, its angry eyes fixed firmly on the imaginary bull's eye painted on your buttocks.

As Mike Daugherty relates on an official Yellowstone National Park web site, two visitors to the park nearly found this out the hard way.

While hiking, the two men spotted a large moose having lunch a few metres from the trail. After taking several pictures, they started taunting the moose—until, without warning, it whirled around and charged at them.

One man managed to climb a tree, while his companion ran for a small cave in some nearby rocks. The angry moose followed the man on the ground, and just as he ducked into the cave, the moose rattled its antlers against the rock.

The moose retreated a few steps, so the man hopped out of the cave. The moose charged again, and the man jumped back inside. The moose retreated, and the man jumped back out. This sequence carried on two or three times before the man in the tree hollered at his friend, "Just stay in the bloody cave and let the moose c alm down!"

"Like hell I'm staying in the cave," the other man retorted. "There's a bear in here."

Another moose near Anchorage, Alaska is famous for making June's Midnight Sun Marathon a little more challenging. A number of participants were running on a path through the woods when a cow moose appeared on the trail ahead of them. Several out-of-state runners who were not accustomed to wildlife attempted to run past her.

The moose snorted, bellowed, and with fire in her eyes, randomly gave chase to the fleeing participants. As the runners abruptly diverted their course and started leaping over forest-floor deadfall, the marathon quickly degenerated into an event more resembling the sixty-metre sprint hurdles.

At least in North America the moose are only ornery and short-tempered. In Norway, the moose get drunk.

I'm not kidding.

While researching this story, I happened upon an intriguing headline in Norway's *Aftenposten* newspaper: "Drunken moose alert in southern Norway." Every autumn, apparently, the resident moose consume large amounts of apples and pears from Norway's fruit trees. The problem is that this unharvested fruit has often fermented, creating high levels of intoxication in the creatures consuming it.

A drunken moose is apparently not unlike a drunken human. Some of them become very good-natured and chummy, like the moose from Buvikasen that decided it wanted some company one morning. It walked onto the porch of one family's home and rang the doorbell. Twice. The man of the house, apparently fearing solicitation of some sort, chose not to answer. The moose eventually gave up and walked away.

Other intoxicated moose, of course, blow steam from their ears and will charge anything at the drop of a hat. It doesn't help that the fermented fruit coincides with the annual fall rut, a time of year when male moose aggressively defend their territory.

A quick scan of related articles in the *Aftenposten* led me to stories about several moose with poor social skills. Some of my favourites were "Moose attacks laundry rack," "Moose breaks into grocery store," and "Moose destroys moose statue in garden."

Another article reported that a moose had charged through the window of a clothing store in Lillehammer. Police believe that the moose, drunk on fermented fruit, may have charged at its own reflection in the store's window.

As strange as these incidents may sound, the most unbelievable headline I came across was "Flying moose lands on car roof."

Investigating further, I learned that Leo Henriksen and his wife were cruising along Norway's Highway 405 in their little red Mazda when, a few kilometres south of Vatnestrom, a 350-kilogram moose flew off a cliff beside the highway and landed on top of the car. It is believed that the female moose was running through the forest when she abruptly came to the edge of the cliff and was unable to put the brakes on.

It's not known if the moose was under the influence of fruit.

I later ran across a similar story from Sergeant Tim Johnson of the Idaho State Police Department, who reported that on US Highway 95, "a cow moose fell off a cliff and onto a passing car."

I don't know about you, but the term "raining cats and dogs" now seems a lot less figurative to me.

Matt Jackson is the president of Summit Studios and publisher of Mugged by a Moose.

Chasing Guinness

Two accidental adventurers paddle a canoe from
Canada to the mouth of the Amazon River.

By Neil Armstrong and Chris Maguire
As told to Allan Kimball

So you want to set a world canoe record? Start off by having no canoeing experience; don't do any research about where you're going; get no sponsorships and go broke before you reach the halfway point. Begin each day late and end early; pick up some frostbite on the Mississippi; portage and battle heat exhaustion with an armed guard across a Colombian desert. Crash into rocky beaches. Get robbed. Dodge bullets, mosquitoes, biting flies, and killer bees. And have an enormous amount of luck.

Above all, don't set out to set a world record.

That's the way we did it. After 9,966,420 paddle strokes, we set a new world record by travelling 13,028 miles by canoe—from Medicine Hat, Alberta to the mouth of the Amazon River at Belem, Brazil.

And it only took us three years.

We know that some paddlers do it differently. Don Starkell—whose 12,181-mile distance record of 1980–82 we broke—had canoed most of his adult life, and planned his trip from Winnipeg to

Belem for ten years before he ever set out. The late Verlen Kruger, perhaps the world's greatest canoeist ever, not only planned his every move over several incredible treks, but even designed and built his own boats to do it. We just drove to a canoe shop and bought what looked good and what folks told us we might need.

Kruger once said that he never carried anything that wasn't essential, and that everything in the canoe had to be the best. We just loaded up until we had five hundred pounds of junk crammed into a seventeen-and-a-half-foot Clipper Tripper, a technique that Neil's father called "fitting ten pounds of shit into a five-pound bag." We had about two inches of freeboard above the water when we first set out on July 12, 1993.

Not much thought went into leaving from Medicine Hat, either. The original plan was to leave from Winnipeg, where Starkell had started his record journey. But if we had retraced his route, all we would have done was match his record. By starting 847 miles farther west, we would break that record.

Not that we actually started in Medicine Hat for that reason, since we had no idea at the time that we would be going on to Brazil. The real reason was that Neil doubted the canoe would survive the eight hundred road miles from Medicine Hat to Winnipeg strapped to a metal rack on the roof of an old car.

Neil believed we could get to Winnipeg on the water. The South Saskatchewan River flows into Lake Diefenbaker, and on the map it looked like the Qu'Appelle River might connect the lake to the Assiniboine River, which flows through Winnipeg.

When Neil called parks officials to see if it was possible, one ranger said that although the Qu'Appelle was usually very low at that time of year, recent flooding might have given it enough water to float on. It might be possible, he told us, but we wouldn't know for certain until we got there.

Originally, we were going to paddle from Manitoba to the mouth of the Rio Grande in Mexico. Everyone made a big deal about our lack of canoeing experience. We thought, What's so difficult about paddling? You just stick the thing in the water, pull it back, and do it again.

By deciding to leave from Alberta, though, we'd already altered the original plan. That many more river miles meant an additional month of paddling. The three-month holiday was suddenly four. Little did anyone know that we would actually be gone for three years.

Even though we had no idea what we were doing, people not in the know assumed we were experts simply because we were doing it. It was unsettling to have bona fide experts ask our advice on paddling matters when we really didn't have a clue. When people asked us why we were doing something a certain way, we often had a difficult time answering. We'd just kind of laugh and turn the question back on them: "Well, how do you do it?"

People wanted us to say it was a lifelong dream. Really, we just wanted to have an adventure, to have a good time and try something a little different. Canoeing is a sport, it's healthy, and it's a great way to meet a lot of new people. That's all that gripped us. And for Chris, it wasn't even that important. His view of the trip was a little summer diversion; just a couple of months floating down a river in Canada.

People were also shocked when we talked about the distances, even when we were still just going to the Rio Grande. When we said we were paddling to Mexico, there would always be looks of horror or amazement. Nobody could quite come to grips with the idea of anyone travelling this distance in a canoe. And why in a canoe? Why not take the bus? Or fly? Why not a big boat? People would sometimes say, "Where's your motor? You're never going to make it."

Even when we were around hardcore canoeists—people who we thought might have been a little more supportive—we'd hear negative comments. Like the time we stopped in Minneapolis, which has a very active canoeing community. Paddlers there told us we'd get frozen in before we got out of Iowa.

We ignored them. It wasn't that we became arrogant; it was just that we'd heard so much advice from so many people warning us about so many dangerous spots in so many rivers—yet most of the time the so-called "trouble spot" would be nothing. Maybe ten years ago, someone's best friend's second cousin would have gone out and overturned a canoe in the dreaded "trouble spot," and from that point on it was to be avoided at all costs. It got to the point where we'd listen to people and be polite, but not pay much attention. We had faith.

For example, we never believed that the Mississippi River could freeze. Wasn't it too big, and didn't it flow too fast? Then somebody showed us photos of barges stuck in the middle of the river and we said, "Yup, it freezes," but we still figured that it wasn't going to happen to us.

At first we were still building up our stamina, so as soon as one of us would suggest a rest stop, the other would instantly agree. That was especially true when we'd spot a "magic" Budweiser sign. We would meet people who would buy us a beer, and sometimes the bartender would even give us a free six-pack. It's not that we would ask for this; strangers just offered it to us all the time—and we're very polite, very British. It's rude not to accept. But that meant we were always stopping early, drinking and telling tales until the bar would close, then not getting back on the river until maybe eleven the next morning.

Through Canada and much of the northern United States, we plied a scheme we called our "water trick" in an effort to get the sort of creature comforts most folks take for granted. Here's how it worked: When we got to a city, we'd look for a safe and comfortable campsite near somebody's yard. Then we'd go up to the house and ask for water. If we knew they couldn't see the canoe, we'd put our life jackets on just so they'd know how we were travelling. Even if we had water, we'd empty it out and go up anyway. We mastered the art of looking pitiful.

The husband would always approach us first, and we'd ask him for some water. After he had given us the water, we'd ask if there was anywhere we could camp. We'd inevitably get talking about the trip, and ultimately get talking about his yard. We'd ask if we could camp there, and he'd go back and check with his wife. The two of us would kind of joke about it, to see how long it would take the wife to come out. We knew that if it took a long time, they wouldn't want us there.

But no one ever refused us. It was just a question of whether or not they'd invite us in for supper. Sometimes we'd spend a little longer putting up the tent, just in case they did. Many times we'd even get a hot shower or an invitation to sleep in a real bed. We'd chuckle about it between ourselves, but we were very appreciative of people's hospitality.

By November, we were on the Mississippi and heading south. The weather was getting very cold and we started to worry that the river might actually freeze. Waking up in the morning, we had to start breaking ice from the tent, packing up, and cracking through ice with our paddles to make headway. We were miserable. Our original plan had called for us to be in Mexico by December, but in mid-December we were only in St. Louis, where we stopped for a couple of days to get warm again.

Chris noticed that his toes were swollen, and that one had developed several interesting colours and a disagreeable smell. We saw a doctor who said that the problem was frostbite. Chris had thought the doctor was just going to inspect the toe, but he pulled out a scalpel and, without warning, began slicing off bits of the toe. He dug deep; you have to get rid of all the bacteria in there.

Then the doctor grabbed Chris's finger and started cutting bits off of that too. Chris's only anaesthetic was his grip on the edge of the bench. Now Chris has something to remember St. Louis by: no top to his big toe, and a rather sensuous indentation on his left index finger.

We arrived in New Orleans in February and spent two weeks recuperating in The City that Care Forgot. We were just in time for Mardi Gras, a celebration neither of us had ever seen. We attended several parades, just watching at first, but it wasn't long before we were diving for those cheap plastic beads like everyone else.

Once we left New Orleans, we had a leisurely paddle along the Intracoastal Waterway to Houston, where we officially became known as "the British Canoe Expedition."

It was here that we decided to try reaching the Amazon. Why not continue into different cultures? We knew that eleven more countries lay ahead, and this would give us the chance to paddle the mighty Amazon River.

Our families back home thought that going on was a great idea. All the cold weather was finally behind us. We'd come about 4,500 miles, with only 9,000 more to go. We were already a third of the way there. So why not? All we needed was a lot of faith and a little bit of ignorance.

Spending time in Houston helped us substantially. First, Bruce Gillan, a canoe shop owner, gave us some much-needed instruction, outfitted us with paddles of the correct size, and helped install a rudder that Verlen Kruger had made for us. We were interviewed on a radio show and read off a list of things we needed, including vaccinations; we got everything we asked for.

We visited the consuls of all the countries we planned to pass through, as well as the British consul, to get letters of safe passage. That idea came from Kruger, and it was probably the smartest thing we ever did. We used those letters all the time, and they got us out of many serious jams. One of them helped save our lives.

When we paddled away from Houston, we had about a thousand dollars each. Not much, but then again, we weren't travelling like tourists. We carried our own transportation and lodging, and food was relatively cheap in Central and South America. Many people thought we had rich families subsidizing our journey, and asked us, "Hey, where's your daddy's gold card?" But every penny we had, we had earned ourselves.

In fact, we ran out of money in Mexico. So we learned how to make hats from palm fronds, and that basically subsidized the rest of the trip. Of course, people weren't just buying the hats because they were wonderful hats—although they were quite stylish and well made. It was a way of giving us donations and getting something back, a souvenir of our adventure, a way for each of them to feel like they were a part of it.

We made considerable money from selling those hats. Every day we'd go to a dock in Cancun where we knew American tourists would arrive. We would then sit in front of the canoe with a big sign behind us that read:

British Canoe Expedition
World Record Challenge
Donations Welcome

We made it all sound quite official so people could see we weren't joking. We'd sit and weave hats, and people would come up and give us money. We got a few hundred-dollar donations, which was surprising. And some people actually liked the hats.

The first time we were robbed was in November along the Mexican coast. A man came up to our tent at about two in the morning, poked us awake with a stick, and demanded, *"Dinero! Dinero!"*

When we stuck our heads out of the tent to see what was going on, he brandished a knife and repeated his demand for money. We'd never seriously thought about robbery before this. Chris shook six pesos out of a bag, hoping the man would leave, but the bandit put his knife to Chris's throat and shouted, *"Mas dinero!"*

We didn't panic. We just kept asking each other how to get out of the situation, speaking in English, while the stranger kept his knife on Chris, now almost piercing his neck.

We wondered if we should use our pepper spray, but thought if we did, the man might panic and stab Chris. We thought of the flare gun and Neil scrambled for it while Chris shouted, "Shoot him! Shoot him!"

But the thief jumped Neil. Neil slapped him in the face and fell away to avoid the knife, his heart thumping and his face flushed with anger. Then he found the pepper spray and gave the robber a full dose. The robber and Neil ran off in opposite directions, the thief turning his attention back to Chris. Neil found the flare gun and tried to load it as Chris doubled back to camp.

In hindsight, it must have looked quite comical, Chris running along in his underwear yelling "Shoot him! Shoot him!" as he was chased by a crazed, knife-wielding *bandito* with a scarf over his head.

Chris, tired of waiting for Neil to save the day, ran down the beach toward a camp of fishermen, trying to remember the Spanish word for "Help!" What he got out was *"Socorro! Socorro! Loco hombre! Bandito!"* The fishermen ran the thief off.

But that robbery was nothing compared to what happened in July near Sandy Bay Sirpi in Nicaragua—the most traumatic event of our lives.

We were camped back in the bush as rain fell. Three men approached in a motorboat, each holding a machete and acting very suspiciously. They asked what was in the canoe, what was in our bags, and demanded that we let them see for themselves. Our bright yellow camera cases held their attention as they shouted something about marijuana and cocaine.

We told them we were waiting for friends who would return any moment, but they demanded to search our bags. They wanted everything we had—our waterproofs, watches, cameras. But we kept refusing. Finally, they told us they would be back and left, heading south down the beach.

We quickly loaded up the canoe and launched through pounding surf. We had two options: paddle far off shore to pass town, or paddle back north and hide in the bush. A storm was fast approaching and they had a motor on their boat, so we knew we couldn't get by them. We headed back up the beach, paddling like crazy against the current and wind, looking for a clearing to hide behind.

We dragged the canoe up the beach and about three hundred yards into a mangrove swamp. Our plan was to wait until dark, then load up and sneak past them.

We sat in the bush whispering, drinking coffee, and eating biscuits. The rain started falling more heavily and we began shivering. Then, as dusk arrived, so did the mosquitoes. We got the ParaWing tarp out and just laid it over us, huddling in the middle of that swamp, getting soaked as the temperature dropped.

Suddenly we heard an explosion. Was it thunder? Or a gun?

We sat up, frozen and waiting with trepidation. Then all hell broke loose. We heard two more gunshots and saw the muzzle flashes, so we kicked off our shelter and ran.

As they chased us, firing their weapons, we got down on our bellies and crawled over mangrove roots and struggled through vines in the blackness. Before long, we couldn't move, and we huddled against the roots in six inches of water. Whispering to one another, we agreed that the expedition was definitely over—even if we survived the night, we'd have no equipment to finish the trip.

We shuddered for hours in the rain, providing the local mosquitoes with a smorgasbord. We hoped the marauders would just take our equipment and leave, because we feared that if they found us, they would kill us.

Every time we thought they had gone, we would hear more gunshots. We moved a few miles down the beach, planning on getting into the surf and drifting in the sea as far as we could go. We moved as well as we could in the total darkness, holding on to each other so we wouldn't get separated.

We stopped once to check the time, but as we switched on the flashlight, more shots were fired, and suddenly we were running for our lives.

Praying that we wouldn't be killed, we headed toward the sound of the surf.

At the water's edge, we slid in like turtles and let the current drag us out. For the next two hours we drifted, swam, and crawled through the surf. Even though it was black, we were far from invisible, because phosphorescence trailed from our shoulders.

At daylight, we dragged ourselves onto the beach, deciding to walk to the nearest town and hope for the best. In the light, we could see that our hands were swollen from mosquito bites and scrapes and cuts.

As we walked into the Miskito Indian town, we were surrounded by villagers. The head man, Garcia Rodriguez, told us that his militia had seen two Colombians on the beach with bags full of cocaine and a shotgun. He had sent his men to search the beach; they had found us and assumed we were the Colombian drug smugglers. They had loaded up our canoe with our equipment and towed it into the village.

We then told our version of the story. We knew we had to be very diplomatic so as not to raise tempers—but we didn't want to become victims either. Still, we were in a Third World country, in a Miskito town in the middle of nowhere, and these people could do anything they wanted with us.

Rodriguez said he was the chief of the Miskitos, and that he possessed a treaty signed by the British in 1915 giving him control over all Miskito people and their lands. His law stated that any vessel must get clearance from him to pass; we hadn't done that. We showed him our letter from the British consul, and once he saw the stamp—the same seal as the one on his precious treaty—he listened to us intently.

Fortunately for us, Rodriguez's Miskitos felt more allegiance to England than to the rest of Nicaragua. After listening to our lengthy explanation of our journey, the chief declared everything a misunderstanding. He and the villagers took us to our canoe—and what a feeling of relief when we saw it and all of our equipment.

We took inventory, and although a few items were missing, most were intact, if a little waterlogged. Our wallets were returned with nothing missing. Nevertheless, the chief did insist that we would have to pay for flashlight batteries and other expenses the militia had incurred during our pursuit, about thirty dollars in all. We joked that maybe we should pay for the bullets they had shot at us, too.

Rodriguez insisted that we stay and recuperate at his house. We saw little choice; our hands were in such terrible condition after our ordeal that we wouldn't be able to paddle for days. Our situation was almost laughable. We were staying in the house of the man who had given orders to shoot us. They fed us, gave us a roof to sleep under, and even became our friends. We stuffed ourselves with turtle meat, rice, bread, and Kool-Aid.

After a few days we continued down the coast, wondering whether we should end our journey. Was this trip worth our lives? We wanted to meet people and have an adventure, not dodge bullets and get robbed and hassled. We decided to continue, but discussed at length measures to avoid a similar situation.

Unfortunately, Columbia would test us again.

In September, we spent sixteen days in Cartagena, Colombia resting and repairing the canoe. The city proved to be everything we'd heard it was—beautiful and relatively safe. But people we met warned us about drug smugglers and Guajira natives, all of whom, apparently, would kill us. Nobody thought we would make it to Venezuela alive.

We called the British embassy and their advice was to stop the expedition immediately because a British diplomat had been kidnapped by terrorists just that week. That wasn't what we wanted to hear, yet we were determined to go on.

We decided to avoid the dreaded Guajira Peninsula. We could portage across it, eliminating 210 miles of paddling through country controlled by smugglers, thieves, and murderers. But the portage meant pulling 500 pounds of gear across 75 miles of desert. We bought a boat trailer and modified it so that we could pull it, then hired an armed guard to escort us across the desert.

The four-day portage eliminated two weeks of dangerous paddling, but it turned out to be the portage from hell. We had never sweated so much in our lives. On the first day, we stopped for water every fifteen minutes, and couldn't walk a full kilometre without a break. Neil was dizzy, had serious headaches, and at times could hardly breathe. He was rapidly approaching heat exhaustion.

Our armed guard was of little help. His mileage calculations were always wrong; he never knew where the rest stops were; and he didn't even have sense enough to wear a hat in the godforsaken heat.

At the end of the first day, after twelve hours of walking, we camped next to a family's house. They invited us in for dinner, but Neil was so exhausted and cramped up that he couldn't stop shaking and couldn't even eat. So he watched a Colombian football match on TV.

We crossed the peninsula successfully, then continued along the coast until the end of December, when we paddled into the Caribbean so we could spend Christmas in Trinidad.

As 1996 began, we entered the Orinoco River, ecstatic to be out of the surf even though we had a thousand miles of upriver paddling ahead of us. For sixteen months, we'd worried about surf and weather. No more.

We saw our first "toninos" on the Orinoco, ugly pink things that look like elephant-man dolphins. Of course, by that point in the journey, we didn't look much better. We each had a multicoloured umbrella up for shade, and our stereo blasted out Cat Stevens, Phil Collins, Hootie & the Blowfish, Van Morrison, and Bob Marley. Regular coffee filters had become too slow, so we drank T-shirt coffee—an acquired taste, a little salty and sweaty to be sure. Whenever we passed people they would laugh and laugh. We were a sight to behold.

The riverbank became a ten-foot vertical wall of green with a canopy of trees and long vines reaching into the water. The sky was filled with squawking macaw parrots. This was an area untouched by gringos. We might have thought we'd found paradise if it hadn't been for the biting black flies, mosquitoes, fire ants, and killer bees.

In June, after we reached the Amazon, the radio batteries suddenly went dead. This disappointed Chris, who had been looking forward to an English football game that was scheduled to be broadcast that afternoon. Not long after the death of the radio, we passed some small three-sided huts built up from the river bank on stilts and decided to stop for water.

Our first surprise was that the small community was Japanese. We never did learn what they were doing in the middle of the Amazon jungle, but although they lived in primitive conditions, they had a power generator. And a satellite dish for their TV. And they were big football fans. Not surprisingly, they just happened to be watching the England/Spain match Chris so wanted to see.

On August 1, 1996, we arrived in Belem, Brazil. We had made it on our own, against the odds. There was no doubting our joy, yet it seemed oddly anticlimactic. Canoeing had been our life for more than three years, and now we didn't have to think about paddling the next day. Or the next.

When we began in Medicine Hat, if we had known everything that we know now—if we had known that we would become the British Canoe Expedition, that we would be written up in dozens of newspapers and magazines in several countries, that we would fill several diaries with notes, that we would set a new world record—we surely would have laughed. Indeed, we might never have done it.

We're glad we didn't know. If we had, we would have felt a lot more pressure. We would have had to be more serious, and we wouldn't have experienced half the things we did. More to the point, we probably wouldn't be in the *Guinness Book of World Records*.

Allan Kimball was writing a weekly paddling column for the Houston Post *when he first met Neil Armstrong and Chris Maguire. He's the author of several books, including* Fun with the Family in Texas *and* The Big Bend Guide. *He is currently working on a trilogy of novels set in the Big Bend of Texas during the 1800s. The first two,* Calamity Creek *and* Woman Hollering Creek, *are already in print, with the third volume,* Second Coffee Creek, *being released in June 2006. Allan is also the editor of* Hill Country Sun *magazine.*

The Glacier

At some point, every man is blessed with luck.

By Robert Sandford

You know you are truly Canadian when you realize that most of the really important moments in your life occurred on or near water in one or all of its remarkable forms. The mere sight of wild water makes Canadians exultant. Many are those whose most formative and cherished moments involve keeping a canoe upright in whitewater, walking in rain along riverbanks, or fishing in local creeks. Or in the case of landlocked prairie people, swimming in rivers shared by hundreds of grazing cattle.

Like many Canadians, my own identity has been greatly established and influenced by water. I think it's fair to say I have an intimate connection with at least one river—the mighty North Saskatchewan.

I should just say that I came to know the North Saskatchewan quite by accident. So perhaps it's fitting that the accident happened at the Columbia Icefield, the birthplace of three of the greatest rivers on the continent: the Athabasca, the Saskatchewan, and the Columbia. This icefield is the largest and highest in the Canadian Rockies, and is one of only two tri-way divides in the world.

Of course, I didn't know any of this when I first came to the Rockies. Like so many young people who come to work in the mountains for a summer, I was young. Twenty to be exact. I had my life all worked out. I was going to have fun for a summer, then return to university in Calgary and graduate with a degree in chemistry. I had picked a wife. I had picked a house. There would be a dog. There would be children. I would drive a wood-panelled station wagon. I was prepared, indeed, for the good life.

Then I fell, unroped, into a crevasse on the Saskatchewan Glacier.

It all began innocently enough. After viewing a dizzying array of mountain climbing slides projected onto the wall at a friend's house, I decided I wanted to become a mountaineer. At least I wanted to be a mountaineer for the summer, before returning to academia and continuing with my "higher" education. And forget half measures; the first trip I embarked on involved traversing across the aforementioned Columbia Icefield. I only had two days off, but hey, I figured that would be more than enough. After all, when you're twenty, how big can an icefield be?

The accident happened while a friend and I descended the Saskatchewan Glacier on the afternoon of the second day. I was so tired that I had altogether given up trying to avoid the big meltwater streams that were coursing across the glacier's broken surface. I was cold, wet, and worn out, and all I wanted to do was get down.

So I took a shortcut.

Unless you have travelled on the surface of a big glacier, it is hard to imagine how much melt can occur on a hot day. There are actually rivers on the surface of the ice. Big rivers. Seeking a direct line, I tried to cross one. This was later deemed to be a mistake. The power of the icy water lifted me up like a bath toy and carried me to the mouth of a yawning crevasse. Then I dropped out of the known world. One moment I was looking at the sun-sparkle of splashing water, a moment later I was in the centre of a waterfall plunging into complete darkness beneath the ice.

The waterfall cascaded down a series of ice lips to join the angry river that flowed beneath the glacier. Never before or since have I heard so many of the exhilarating sounds water can make. Here I was inside a planetary artery examining firsthand what water does to the world, and all I could think, believe it or not, were unappreciative thoughts.

It wasn't long before I realized I had another little problem. Only a few inches separated the top of the underground river from the roof of the ice. In darkness, I kept smashing into boulders and scraping against the underside of the glacier. Just as the shock and wonder were beginning to wear off—just as calm was about to give way to sheer terror—the strangest thing happened. The ice above me began to glow.

At first it was a faint green, but as the river swept me onward, the glow intensified. Green gradually merged into a pale blue. I noticed then, for the first time, that rocks were hanging out of a ceiling made entirely of light. It is, without question, one of the most beautiful things I have ever seen. Then I popped out of the glacier into sunshine and was washed into the full flood of the North Saskatchewan River.

And that's where my problems really began.

People often ask me if the accident changed anything, and I have to acknowledge that it most certainly did. The accident changed everything. From that day forward, my life flowed toward unexpected ends. I never did finish my chemistry degree or get that wood-panelled station wagon. Perhaps more importantly, I now realize I have spent the rest of my life trying to prevent my own culture from carrying me downstream and away from the luminous glory of that sub-glacial light.

Robert Sandford is the author of several books and is Chair of the United Nations "Water for Life" Initiative in Canada. He contends that glaciers are important to our water supply and quite beautiful, but recommends viewing them from above ground. He lives in Canmore, Alberta.

Savvy Nomads

The Arabian Desert still holds a few surprises.

By Stacey Fitzsimmons

It was six long and sweaty hours before my boyfriend Craig and I had hiked, climbed, and scrambled our way to the top of the "Stairway to Heaven" pass, which lay on the dusty border between the United Arab Emirates and Oman's Musendam Peninsula.

Although the view from the top was most certainly heavenly, the pathway to get there was not. Half our day had been spent slowly plodding up a loose scree slope, where each step up produced a small rock slide that carried us half a step back down. The other half of the day was spent in sheer terror as we clutched crumbling rock ledges and prayed that the stacked rocks we were climbing wouldn't topple. When we stood at the top of the pass, however, looking down on the lights of the town where we had started that morning, I admitted proudly that the view was well worth the effort, despite the terrifying, ridiculously hot climb.

I was in the United Arab Emirates for two weeks in the spring of 2004 to visit Craig, who was working a contract at the Al Ain airport. Neither of us had ever been to the Middle East before, so we were excited to travel and explore the area. I'm an avid hiker, and Craig liked to accommodate me, so one of our first activities was to escape the city of Al Ain for two days in the mountains.

Lack of rain ensures sunny skies in Oman, but planning for drinking water can be challenging. At home, I'm used to hiking or paddling in areas where fresh water is plentiful. I've never had to worry about packing fresh water for a hike. So it was with serious consideration that I tried to estimate how much water we would need for our overnight camping trip. Once I'd done the calculations, I realized our packs would weigh more than fifty pounds each if we carried that much water. Water is bloody heavy! So I decided my calculations must be wrong and foolishly cut our supply of water by one third. I figured if we got going early enough on the second day and down-climbed back to our car by early afternoon (where we would stash extra water), we would be fine.

During our climb, we noticed there weren't many people living in the mountains—and for good reason. It's almost impossible to grow anything in the barren, scorched terrain. Those who do live there have adapted by becoming nomadic farmers. No, they don't uproot their farms and carry them on their backs. Rather, they move between several small farms, tending and watering each parcel of land just enough to produce food.

These farms (some of them not much bigger than large household gardens) are found in the most unbelievable locations: perched on mountain ledges, at the top of ridges, and snuggled between boulders along high valley floors. In fact, the path we were following was once a trail used by farmers to reach arable land at the top of the pass. Now deemed too steep and dangerous, the trail for the most part has been abandoned. Having climbed it, I can understand why.

Sure enough, at the top of the trail we found a small garden enclosed by a stone wall, with a small, open-roofed rock hut to one side. A few green things peeked out of the dry brown earth and some chickens wandered nearby. There was no road, no water, and no electricity.

But there was one inhabitant. While we stood there catching our breath, we noticed a man walking toward the hut from the other side of the mountain, leading a donkey and carrying a bale of hay on his head. We waved at him, marvelling at the tenacious hold this man, and other farmers like him, had on the land. He waved back, but we were too far away to strike up a conversation. We were self-conscious about the few words of Arabic we knew anyway, so we continued on our way, looking for a flat piece of ground to camp for the night.

Such little rain or insect life means there's no need for a tent in Arabia—a good thing, given all the water we were carrying. The only possible "campsite" we found was a pair of small ledges jutting out from the mountainside. Craig and I each took a ledge, carefully placing rocks on the exposed sides to ensure we didn't roll off the mountain in our sleep. As I'm sure you can imagine, it was not a very good night's slumber. The one redeeming part of the night came at dusk, when the man from the small farm we had seen earlier started to play an instrument. Life in the mountains must be lonely at times, and the music seemed to tell the story of that loneliness. Craig and I sat up late into the night, listening to the farmer play his simple, heartfelt tune.

We woke at dawn to take advantage of the cool morning hours on our descent. From the description in our trail book, the hike should have taken about four or five hours, so we estimated we would be down by noon. Well, by noon we were still four thousand feet off the valley floor and quickly running out of both water and good humour. The trail was unmarked, so the only way to discern the path from the rest of the rocky slope was to find where the rocks had been worn shiny and black by thousands of footsteps passing over them. This had worked well for our ascent the day before when the options were limited, but once we got onto more level ground on the way down, we found that we completely lost the trail. We spent the entire morning crawling and cursing our way over sharp, car-sized boulders, and we were no closer to finding a trail to the foot of the mountain. Things did not look good.

Finally, we spotted two small farms squeezed onto a ledge halfway down the mountain. Two men lounged in the shade of a scraggly tree, trying to sleep off the midday sun. They were obviously smarter than Craig and me—taking refuge from the ridiculous desert heat. Despite our potentially dangerous situation, I had no idea how to approach or communicate with them, so we decided that as long as we kept going down, we would be fine. We waved to the men and started to climb down over their ledge onto the next steep boulder slope. Thank goodness they called out to us.

We walked over to their little patch of shade. The farm was a bit greener than the one we had seen on the pass. It had an elaborate irrigation system with dozens of cement troughs directing water from the mountainside to their farms. It apparently worked quite well, since the farms looked relatively productive.

We tried as best we could to indicate that we were trying to get to the valley bottom. The men seemed to understand, and made motions for us to follow them. We assumed they were going to point us in the right direction, and were infinitely grateful for their help. Instead, they escorted us for the next two and a half hours, all the way to the valley floor, following their well-used but almost invisible mountain trails. About halfway down, we passed a dark stagnant pond hidden under an overhang, which must have been the only permanent water source in the area.

The most amazing thing about the men was their speed and agility. Obviously accustomed to traversing the mountains, they motored along in their flip-flops, maintaining a quick but steady pace. The older man, who looked to be in his seventies, offered several times to carry our packs, but we declined. The younger man might have been his son, since they both shared the same easy smile and loping gait.

We walked for about half an hour at a time, and then stopped for five minutes to catch our breath. I suspect these breaks were solely for our benefit, since our two guides didn't look the least bit hot or tired. On the other hand, Craig and I were dying. It's a humbling experience to be outpaced by a seventy-year-old man wearing flip-flops and a *dishdasha* (a long white cotton dress-like suit).

As much as possible, we tried to communicate with our guides during these brief rest stops. Through short words and liberal use of hand signals, we learned that they had several farms in this mountain range. However, we thought we must have misunderstood them when they indicated they were returning to the small farm at the top of the pass later that evening. They were quick, but it was nearing four in the afternoon, and we weren't even at the bottom of the valley yet. Besides, could it be true that they went four or five hours out of their way just to lead us safely down the mountain? Our respect for these men continued to grow.

We finally reached the valley floor where our car was parked. We offered them some money in thanks for their generosity, which started a give-and-take dance that went on for a few minutes—they at first refused to take it, but we insisted. We in the Western world have cars and cell phones, and these nomadic farmers have nothing but their feet to travel on through these dusty mountains, squeezing a marginal living from the arid soil. Eventually they relented, and graciously accepted the money.

That was when we were treated to another surprise. We had expected the men to turn around and return to their mountain home via the same path we had just descended. Instead, they walked a few metres beyond our car to a large white truck and hopped in. As they drove away, we could see the younger man pluck his cell phone from the seat and start dialling a number. Apparently, there's more than one way to climb a mountain in the Arabian Desert.

Stacey Fitzsimmons is currently working on a PhD in International Business at Simon Fraser University in Vancouver. She specializes in cross-cultural management, and contends that getting lost in foreign countries is the best way to study exotic lands and their peoples.

Death by Vacation

The curse of being married to an adventurous husband.

By Leslie Bamford

"I found the perfect vacation," says Bob, waving the travel section of the newspaper. "With scuba diving included."

"I don't know how to scuba dive." I speak slowly and deliberately because of my husband's uncanny ability to tune me out when I am talking to him.

"You could take a course this spring at the pool," he says. "They teach you to use a snorkel and overcome your fear of breathing underwater."

"Sounds like drowning to me."

"It's very safe once you're trained. And you can finally get some use out of that wetsuit I bought you."

"It doesn't fit."

"How do you know?"

"Being married to you has made me fat."

"Wetsuits stretch."

"Oh, so you think I'm fat…"

"I didn't say that," he backtracks quickly. "I just think you'd love the things you can see underwater."

I look at Bob more closely. Sure enough, he has a demented

look in his eye. The look he always gets just before he tries to kill me on vacation.

*   *   *

The warning signs about Bob's search for adventure were apparent when we were first dating. One night at a trendy restaurant, the topic of taking a trip together came up. "Do you dream about going anywhere special?" I asked, wanting to know more about him.

"Mars."

"Pardon?"

"Mars would be nice. Somewhere no one else has been. Off the beaten track, full of mystery."

"You're kidding, right?"

"You mean you wouldn't go to Mars?"

"Definitely not."

"Why not?"

"It's too far. It takes too long. I would miss my friends. The spacesuits would be uncomfortable…"

"But think of the views. I'd go at the drop of a hat."

"So, hypothetically, if I were your partner, you'd go to Mars without me? Be gone for years? Is that what you're saying?" My voice shot up.

"And you would want me to stay here and live a humdrum life when we could go on the adventure of a lifetime? Is that what you're saying?" His voice shot up to match mine.

The waitress came by, saw the looks on our faces and backed off.

"I just can't believe anyone would turn down the opportunity to go to Mars." Bob's face turned dark, the smile in his eyes fading like a lunar eclipse.

"I don't want to spend the prime of my life going to the bathroom in a spacesuit," I said, not realizing that this statement would come back to haunt me throughout our relationship. To Bob, it represented my fixation with things practical, my resistance to change, my cold feet compared to his wanderlust. To me, the Mars argument represented the first time I was exposed to Bob's visionary side, to his love of ideas (possible or otherwise), and to his penchant for dreaming.

We drove home avoiding eye contact.

In the morning the phone rang. "This is Bob. Calling from Mars."

I paused, trying to think of something smart to say and not coming up with anything better than, "Hi. How's the view?"

"Not so good. There's all this red dust around. And it's kind of lonely up here. So I'm coming back. Want to do something this afternoon? We could go to the planetarium."

"Sounds more my speed."

We never did make it to the planetarium, but we made it to the altar. Mars is on hold. My goal every summer since then is to stay within my comfort zone on holidays—take my laptop along, get some writing done, enjoy a little fresh air and pleasant scenery. Typical middle-aged things like that. Instead, our vacations seem to evolve into death-defying activities, no matter how blandly they develop from discussions over Australian Chardonnay and Yugoslavian Riesling in the safety of our home in January.

The scuba diving holiday didn't pan out. Bob recognized that it was a losing cause trying to coerce a woman who has gained weight to wear a rubber suit that no longer fits. So he gave up. Instead, he began to lobby for a sailboat. He dragged me through a myriad of marinas around the Great Lakes for several summers, ogling boat after boat, chatting up boat owners, poring over catalogues, surfing boating sites on the Internet. The more interested he became, the more my heart sank like a ship in a bad storm. Not that I am afraid of water. In fact, I can swim quite well. But not to shore from the middle of Lake Ontario. If you get my drift.

My first experience with sailing was inauspicious to say the least. Despite the Mars conversation, we were engaged by then and vacationing at South Carolina's Myrtle Beach. I was lying under a beach umbrella feeling safe and secure when Bob spied an outfit renting catamarans down the shoreline from our hotel.

"Let's rent one of those Hobie Cats this afternoon," said Bob. His blue eyes were lighting up like a halogen lamp.

"I'm sure they're too expensive," I replied, hoping to divert him by appealing to his sense of fiscal responsibility.

"To hell with the cost, we're on vacation."

"Do you know how to sail a catamaran?"

"Sailing is sailing—Hobie Cats, Sunfish, boats with fixed hulls. It's no sweat, you'll love it."

"They're probably all booked up."

"Let's go and see."

Before I could think of another objection, he grabbed my hand and led me down the beach.

To my dismay, the catamarans were not all booked. One ratty craft was lying on the beach beside a hut that had half its thatched roof missing. The boat, if you could call it that, was leaning at a peculiar angle, one pontoon sticking up like the leg of a dog taking a leak.

Bob exchanged money with a tanned beach bum sporting tattoos of ferocious marine life on his upper arms. He said some technical things to Bob about handling the Cat in the strong Atlantic surf. I tried to compute the instructions but they sounded like a foreign language. All I understood was something about the surf making it difficult to return to shore.

"Are there sharks out there?" I asked.

Instead of answering, the beach bum handed us two soiled orange life jackets. We put them on. Everything was happening too fast. I felt powerless to stop the progress of my own demise.

The beach bum helped Bob drag the Hobie to the edge of the beach. Following directions, I climbed onto a trampoline-like mat that was strung with frayed rope between the pontoons. It was dirty and worn. The sail flapped back and forth, swinging dangerously near my head. Before I could voice my final objection, the beach bum and Bob began running through the surf, one on each side of the craft, propelling me toward the horizon. Waves crashed over me as the Hobie bucked and slapped the water.

Bob leaped onto the mat beside me, beaming.

The beach bum returned to his hut to smoke whatever he smoked and wait for another suicidal customer.

"Isn't this great?" Bob yelled above the roar of the waves as he pulled on some lines hanging from the ragged sail. I stared at him in disbelief as my stomach began to register the fact that we were no longer on terra firma. Bob appeared transported to a divine realm.

I discovered in a hurry that Hobie Cats are extremely uncomfortable. There are no handholds, just the edge of the frame. To stay aboard, I had to kneel on all fours on my side of the mat, keeping my head down to avoid decapitation as we came about and caught a gust of wind, careening out to sea.

"Yahoo!" cried Bob.

I looked back. The beach bum's hut was no longer visible. I couldn't believe how quickly we had sailed away from shore. All that stood between me and death by sharks or drowning (or both) was the ugly mat against which my nose was plastered.

"Coming about!" cried Bob.

The Hobie turned, shuddered, and came to an almost complete stop like a dying whale as Bob and I scrambled around each other, changing sides on the mat so he could remain in the position of skipper. I felt nauseous, bile rising in my throat. Just then a strong gust of wind caught the sail and we took off again, screaming across the waves on one pontoon.

"We're leaning over too far!" I screamed, clinging to the mat. "I'm falling out!"

"You're fine, just hang onto the edge," said Bob as he pulled in the sail to bring the Hobie's pontoon back down. "And it's heeling, not leaning. You're a sailor now. You have to learn the lingo."

"I'm no sailor. Take me back to shore."

"Let's come about one more time. I think I know how to sail this thing now," Bob said.

"What do you mean NOW?" I yelled. "You said you've sailed before."

"Not catamarans. The ride is a little rougher than I imagined."

"Jesus, man, this is a fine time to tell me."

"Don't worry, we're fine. Coming about!"

Before I could object, the sail whipped over my head and Bob began to crawl over me. To save myself from being crushed to death by a large man on a scruffy mat, I had no choice but to scuttle to the other side of the Hobie.

Bob turned the boat on a thirty-degree angle to the waves and trimmed the sail. The Hobie transformed from a dying whale to a perfectly balanced craft heading for the coast of Africa. My nausea subsided as we stopped wallowing in every trough and slapping hard against every wave. The sun began to dry my swimsuit. I released my death grip on the frame and sat up on the mat, daring to look around.

The expanse of blue water was dotted with whitecaps that sparkled in the afternoon sun. The beach was a thin brown line behind us. Puffy fair-weather clouds lined the horizon. It was suddenly very quiet as Bob's grey hair blew in the wind. He turned and smiled at me, his face radiant with joy.

"See how beautiful it is out here?"

I nodded, speechless with residual fear and the influx of sensory data. We sailed for a while in silence before coming about again. I had the hang of it now, ducking under Bob at the right time, so we wallowed less and skimmed over the waves in the opposite direction without stalling.

I felt myself smiling, despite my fear. "The waves don't look as sinister as they did a few minutes ago," I said to Bob.

"That's because we aren't fighting them any more. That's what sailing is all about. Being in the groove. One with the rhythm of nature."

We came about again, enjoying one last ride toward the horizon, then turned back like pros and headed toward the shore.

It was soon apparent, however, that sailing in the same direction as the swells, some of them four feet or more, was a whole new challenge. The craft was hurtled forward at breakneck speed by each crest, only to sink into a trough and nearly stall before the next wave shot us forward again. I reclaimed my death grip on the edge of the trampoline. Nausea returned. I suddenly found myself hoping that my mother would come and save me, which was illogical since she was prone to seasickness, hated boats, and had been dead for five years.

The shoreline seemed to be rushing toward us.

"Do you know how to do this?" I yelled at Bob.

"Hell, no."

"I thought Shark Man told you how."

"He said something about it."

"WHAT?"

It was too late for conversation. We were hurtling toward the beach high atop a rogue wave the size of a house (or so it seemed from my face-down vantage point on the mat). Bob let out the sail and pulled hard on the rudder, and we skimmed through the shallow water and up onto the beach for a perfect ten-point landing like he'd done it a thousand times.

As I climbed off the Hobie, I realized that my back was killing me, my legs were shaking, and my stomach was still churning.

Shark Man came down to meet us, took our life jackets, and dragged the Hobie unceremoniously up the beach toward the hut.

"Nice landing, bro," he said over his shoulder to Bob.

Bob grinned and put his arm around my shoulders as we started walking along the beach toward the hotel.

"You did great out there. I'm buying you a martini."

"I think some Maalox might go down better."

"That'll pass once you get used to sailing," Bob said.

"I'll never get used to sailing," I replied.

"That Hobie was damn uncomfortable. But you'll love a real sailboat once we buy one."

"I'm never going sailing again," I said, meaning every word.

"Of course you are." He squeezed my elbow to emphasize his words.

Back home from the beach, I contemplated this unwelcome new twist in our relationship and wondered if I should marry Bob.

Co-ownership of a boat would be a huge commitment, like sharing a dog or a pony. I weighed the situation, taking into account my pitiful lack of knowledge about boating, my fear of drowning, my desire to stay inside my comfort zone, and the expression of ecstasy on Bob's face when he was out on the open water. I think it was the look that tipped the scales. I decided to stay in the relationship.

I had no way of knowing that by marrying Bob, I would eventually learn to sail a thirty-four-foot sailboat. That being with him would force me to overcome my fear of heights and my fear of flying. Not to mention my fear of being lost in the woods, struck by lightning, frozen to death, and eaten by wild beasts. Marriage is not for the faint of heart. Especially when you marry someone who wants to go to Mars.

I figured that once we were married, I could talk him out of buying a boat. I had a lot to learn about Bob.

*   *   *

"Here's an ideal vacation," said Bob, a year after our wedding. Snow was falling softly outside the window of our living room. "We could hike the Long Trail from the Canadian border to Massachusetts next summer."

He smiled across the coffee table.

"There's no way we could go that far in two weeks." My feet began to ache just thinking about it.

"We could do one section, then."

"Where would we sleep?" I asked.

"In hostels."

"With sweaty hikers who snore? No, thanks."

"We could commune with nature."

"I'd probably catch poison ivy. Or Lyme disease."

"The trail goes over Mount Mansfield, the highest peak in Vermont. That'd be the best part to hike."

"There are mountain lions in Vermont. And bears."

"We could buy a sailboat instead." He looked at me slyly.

Put that way, drowning didn't sound so bad.

Leslie Bamford is a native of Montreal who always enjoyed writing letters, term papers, memos, and grocery lists. The light finally dawned and she began creative writing. She is currently working on a book about living with a wacky husband, a feisty black cat, and her mother's ghost. She lives in Kitchener, Ontario.

Eel of a Good Time

What happens when a scuba lesson turns ugly?

By Boris King

As our Jeep slowly edged down a steep dirt trail on the north side of Lanai Island, my friend Henry and I bounced around like popcorn in a frying pan. This place we were driving to certainly wasn't your average tourist destination. Descending to the rocky beach, I wondered briefly if a rookie scuba diver like myself should be tackling a night dive in a place like this. There wasn't a soul around, and the only signs of life were the lights of Maui twinkling across the channel in the far distance.

But Henry was determined, so—using the Jeep's headlights— we put on our dive gear and prepared for our underwater adventure in the dark. I shivered while Henry set up our lantern on the beach. What was under that inky blackness? This seemed more and more like a serious endeavour.

Scuba diving was not something I had ever done before I met Henry. Sailing was my passion. In fact, my family and I had been sailing to Australia from Vancouver when we met Henry at a marina in Maui. He was a friendly fellow, and we immediately took a shine to him and his family.

Henry was an experienced diver and spear fisherman, and one morning he stopped by to inquire about chartering our boat for three weeks. The only catch was that he wanted a diving partner on the charter—but if I accepted, he would teach me everything he knew.

Henry went as far as to buy two complete sets of dive equipment, one for him and one for me: wetsuits, lead weights, buoyancy compensators, air tanks, regulators, and spear guns. He also bought me a complete underwater learning system—so I would be ready to write my scuba exam by the end of the three-week charter. I didn't realize at the time that those scuba lessons would serve me for years to come. Learning the sport taught me not only how to dive, but also the art of mind and body control.

Henry must have invested some serious time in doing his homework before arriving on board, because he had a definite idea where we should go and what we should do. Thank God, because I didn't have a clue!

Henry had heard that spearfishing was good on the north side of Lanai Island, and that the best fishing was at night. As soon as I heard the words "night" and "dive" in the same sentence, I began to wonder if I was getting in over my head.

At least Henry was a stickler for safety, which calmed my nerves somewhat. One of the best investments he'd made was a barn-style lantern that we could leave on the beach as a reference point. This one simple purchase, as it turned out, would save our skins. The strong currents running along Lanai's north shore can easily carry divers out to sea without them realizing it, and at night, we might never have found our way back to the island.

My chest tightened with anticipation as we walked out into the darkness and with very little ceremony plunged into the black ocean. Suddenly, I wasn't so keen to swim far from the beach. The only reason I followed was because by this point, we were descending deeper and not communicating; since I couldn't get Henry's attention to express my fear, I just swam after him and hoped for the best. I began hyperventilating, but realized that if I continued like that, I would quickly run out of oxygen.

"Calm down," I told myself over and over again. "Calm down."

Henry, swimming ahead in the beam of my dive flashlight, eventually turned around and made a "thumbs up" signal, wanting to know if I was all right. I returned the gesture. I was starting to regain control and I didn't want to ruin his adventure. I relaxed as my mind became focused not on my fear, but on the verdant sea life that appeared in the narrow sweep of light from the flashlight.

Henry started fishing immediately. He got lucky, spearing a grouper and a couple of other fish I didn't recognize. Then he zeroed in on a lobster.

I wasn't so capable. I'm sure I was a sorry sight as I tried to operate my Hawaiian sling in the Pacific's darkness. It took all the coordination and concentration I could muster to point the light at a fish, aim, and release the sling, all the while fighting the current with my feet floating over my head. Now I felt thankful that it was night, so that Henry couldn't see my underwater acrobatics. As my spear bounced repeatedly off the coral heads, I was shocked at how little control I had over my aim.

Henry had much better success. He gallantly swung by me and stuffed a couple of his fish into the empty net hanging from my weight belt, then pointed up to indicate that he wanted to surface.

Sure enough, we had drifted westward. Our lantern on shore was barely visible, and we could hardly see the outline of the island. Wow! It was so dark that without that little twinkle on the beach, we wouldn't have had a clue where we were. We decided to dive again, but this time we would swim against the current along the ocean floor, where it wasn't as strong.

No sooner had we descended to the bottom than Henry spotted what I thought was an enormous shark swimming sluggishly by. (Later, Henry would argue that it was "only" six to eight feet long.) Immediately, Henry darted behind a large brain coral head—and you can be sure I was right behind him. We turned our dive lights off.

All I could hear was the pounding of my heart and the gurgle of air bubbles each time I exhaled. I was terribly frightened in that blackness. All I could envision was that shark taking a chomp out of us—we would never even see it coming.

Henry turned his light back on momentarily and we watched, relieved, as the uninterested shark vanished into the darkness. It may have disappeared, but in my mind it was right behind me, stalking me, swimming in that dark area where it couldn't be seen. As we swam along the ocean floor, I acted like a suspicious gangster, peering over my shoulder every few seconds to check if something was following us.

Under a large ledge I finally spotted a sizable fish, so I decided to spear it. Inside a hole within a coral head I could see its large tail and body pointing deep into the cavern—normally, fish keep their tails to the back of the hole with their heads facing the entrance so they can watch for predators. I praised my good fortune, cocked the sling as tightly as I could, and came as close to the fish's body as possible to ensure I wouldn't miss. I released the spear, and it penetrated my target dead-on.

Suddenly, a hard tug on the spear pulled me forward, slamming my face against the coral head. My feet floated upward and for a moment I was rendered completely off-balance; before I could react, my legs were high over my head. Whatever was at the end of my spear was big, and it was determined to pull me into the hole behind it. But I was equally determined not to let it get away. I hung desperately onto the spear with both hands.

Visibility soon became a problem—my kicking stirred up the sand, making the water cloudy. On top of that I had lost control of my dive light. It was now dangling by its strap around my wrist, flashing every which way as the fish yanked me to and fro. I couldn't see anything. While I tried to regain control and plant my feet on the bottom, the fire coral scratched my bare legs, which felt like they were being burned by hot coals.

As the fish continued to tug at my spear like a big dog trying to yank a stick out of my hand, I managed to get my fins back on the bottom and regain some control. My face and knees were still leverage points, but at least now I had a firm grip on my spear. I used my leg to wedge the flashlight against the coral head with the beam shining to my left. With my hands deep in the hole, grasping the spear, I saw movement through the cloudy water. I didn't realize what was happening until a huge set of snake-like jaws appeared just inches from my left arm and tried to take a bite out of it.

After a second, I realized that the action of the ominous head on my left corresponded with the tugs of my spear. Those threatening jaws were apparently connected to the tail my spear was embedded in.

Frozen with fear, I realized that I had speared a huge moray eel that had been resting in a two-ended hole.

My fear amplified. Just a couple of days before, I had read about moray eels in a book on tropical fish—about how they hunt from their holes, attacking their prey, which sometimes includes unsuspecting divers. The eels lock their victims in their jaws like pit bulls until they finally drown or bleed to death. Not a nice way to go!

Needless to say, I was in a predicament. If I gave an inch, those snapping jaws moved that much closer to my arm—but I was reluctant to pull too hard, as I envisioned the spear ripping loose and freeing the eel. I yanked on the spear and gained some ground, enough to buy a bit of time to look for Henry.

Consumed with his own pursuits, Henry hadn't been aware that I had fallen behind. Now I could see him in the distance, swimming toward me.

By the time Henry arrived, I was exhausted. He quickly assessed the situation and sent a clean shot through the eel's neck. Using his fins, he pinned its head against the sand and pulled out the diving knife strapped to his leg, then punctured the creature's head with a single, swift stroke.

Adrenaline rushed through me as I watched Henry drag the lifeless eel out of the hole from the other end, my spear still embedded in its tail. It looked like a huge snake, and was so big that Henry barely managed to stuff it into his dive bag. He was visibly delighted with our catch—I remembered that he had wanted to catch an eel and either smoke or barbecue it. Eel was a prized delicacy in Hawaii.

Henry pointed toward the beach and, like a football coach, indicated a time out. I couldn't have been more delighted.

As I followed him, I could see fish blood streaming out of his dive bag, which now made me worry about the shark we had seen earlier. Clenching my teeth, I followed slightly behind and about ten feet to Henry's left. Even though I was not an experienced diver, I had a notion that it was not the cleverest thing to have a dive net full of bleeding fish strapped to your waist.

A large coral formation loomed in front of us. Henry, who was now three or four metres to the right of me, and as much ahead, decided to swim around it, whereas I decided to ascend about the same distance and swim over it. The beauty and the colours of this particular coral head mesmerized me as I glided up its wall.

That's when the worst of my nightmares suddenly came true.

Without warning, a powerful sea creature charged me from out of the darkness, knocking me backward. In shock, I let out the loudest scream of fear the sea has ever heard.

I was in shock, unable to feel the pain from a bite or any other injury. I had lost control of my flashlight when the animal first struck; now the light once again dangled from the strap around my wrist and flashed wildly in all directions. I kicked and shoved, trying to repel the attacker, but to no avail. It kept coming at me, forcing me down toward the bottom.

I tried to inhale a breath of air, only to realize that my panic-stricken scream had blown the regulator right out of my mouth. A rush of water surged into my lungs and I started choking and gagging.

With my right hand, I frantically flailed around for the regulator, while I used my left hand to shove the aggressive attacker away. It didn't seem to matter how hard I struggled and tried to escape; the vicious creature stayed on top of me every inch of the descent.

That's when I felt my spear gun slip off my right arm. I cursed my carelessness—that weapon had been my only hope of survival. A few seconds later the oxygen tank on my back slammed against the bottom of the ocean. Now I was helpless. The creature had me pinned.

As I continued to struggle in the blackness, the regulator dropped into the palm of my right hand, just as if somebody had shoved it there. I quickly stuck it into my mouth, and even though I had swallowed and choked on some salt water, I managed to get myself breathing again.

When I began to regain some form of control, I was puzzled by the fact that I could not feel any pain. Then it dawned on me that the animal hadn't bitten me … yet. With both my hands now free to fight, I grabbed my assailant and tried to shove it off me. To my surprise, it did not feel like what I imagined a shark would feel like.

Using all my strength, I shoved the creature away, but it came charging back. Finally, I managed to shine the light on my attacker and reveal its identity.

It was not a shark at all, but a giant sea turtle.

With a sigh of relief, I tried frantically to wiggle my way out from under the turtle. As I slithered along the bottom, kicking up a huge cloud of soot, I realized that the turtle actually seemed to be more interested in the source of the light than in me. I turned the flashlight off, and—just like that—the onslaught ended.

For a few seconds, I lay there motionless and listened to the deafening thumps of my heartbeat. When I turned the light back on and quickly scanned the depths, I saw the confused turtle in the distance, disappearing into the darkness.

There was no sign of Henry, so I assumed he was waiting for me on the other side of the coral head. Still frightened and confused, I searched for my spear. I wanted to have it in my hand, cocked and ready to fire.

Once I found it, I dashed in the direction of the coral head, this time circling around it. Henry wasn't there.

Hyperventilating, I kicked hard and continued in the general direction I had last seen him swimming. It seemed like forever before I finally saw his flashlight shining in the distance.

In my eagerness to catch up with Henry, I didn't care how fast I was breathing, how much air I was using, or how many sharks might be chasing me. I was fixated on the tiny light way off in the distance. I was about forty feet behind him when he finally stopped, turned around, and waited for me to catch up. Of course, he couldn't actually see me; all he could see was my light.

He stuck his hand out and made a diver's "everything okay?" signal with his fingers. Realizing that he didn't have a clue about what had just happened, I shone my light on my fingers and showed the "okay" sign.

My nerves slowly settled down as Henry led the way back toward the beach. Just as I started to relax, however, I noticed that inhaling through my regulator seemed harder than usual. I checked to see if the air hose was kinked, but it seemed to be straight, so I tried to clear the regulator, reaching over my shoulder to open the valve on the tank some more. It was already open all the way.

My mind raced. I remembered Henry teaching me to look often at my air pressure gauge to ensure I didn't run out of air. Sure enough, when I checked it, the gauge wasn't at the empty mark ... but below it.

My heart jumped, beating wildly. Every time I tried to draw a breath, the regulator made a clacking sound. My lungs felt like they were going into spasms. I craved air desperately.

For the third time that night, I was in trouble.

Luckily, in my panic, I remembered Henry's warning never to ascend with lungs full of air. So I closed my eyes, exhaled the little air I had left, and slowly started to kick with my fins.

The fifty-foot ascent seemed never-ending. I didn't know what was going to happen first—if my lungs were going to implode or if I was going to pass out.

Finally I broke the surface, still clenching the regulator between my teeth. I spat it out and gasped at the air, flooding my lungs with fresh oxygen.

To my amazement, I could see our lantern on the shore straight ahead of me, just a few hundred feet away. As soon as my breathing normalized, I made a beeline for shore. I wanted to get out of this death trap called the Pacific.

Henry surfaced in front of me, and we struggled to walk out of the water toward the lantern as if we had been together all along. I was sure running out of air was a big no-no, so I didn't even mention it. Henry was preoccupied anyway, obviously delighted with our catch, and he rattled on about the feast we would soon be enjoying.

Back on the beach, we turned on the Jeep's headlights to examine our catch. The eel's colours were illuminated in the light; I was shocked at how much smaller it looked out of the water, even though it still drove shivers down my spine.

In his kind and humble way, Henry couldn't stop talking about my catch as he piloted the Jeep back up the steep embankment. My mind drifted as I recalled the events of the past few hours. Just thinking about everything that had happened made my body shake and tremble involuntarily. I was thankful that Henry was talking and the Jeep was rocking so that he wouldn't notice. Henry continued to plan our future night diving endeavours out loud, never realizing that while he talked, I was thinking of how to ensure that we would never go on a night dive again.

The next day, Henry invited a few friends over for a little afternoon barbecue of fish, lobster, and eel. It seemed like the whole island showed up. They brought food and drinks of their own, but the highlight was definitely our barbecued eel.

Hawaiians love eel, but apparently, not many divers dare to spear it. They fussed over me a great deal, treating me with a lot of respect and referring to me as "Captain Courageous." I had never experienced that kind of treatment before, and my spirits soared to unprecedented heights.

Although I felt uncomfortable, I decided to keep quiet. They would never know that it was not my courage that had helped me spear the eel, but rather my ignorance and lack of experience. I wouldn't have gone near that eel if I had known what it was.

At least it was delicious!

Boris and Shirley King, co-authors of the book The Unsinkable Spirit: In Search of Love, Adventure and Riches, *have devoted their lives to adventures at sea. Their second book,* The Unsinkable Spirit: Falling Up, *is due for release in early 2007. Captain King is also an adventure keynote speaker. For booking information, visit www.borisking.com.*

The Night I Bagged Twelve Chicks

Our roving author is accused of being "cheep!"

By John Marriott

It is two-thirty in the morning. I am exhausted, yet exhilarated. I have just spent the last three hours in the cold and the dark chasing chicks around on a deserted islet on the Queen Charlottes, loving every minute of it.

It will go down in my mind as a night of legend—the night I bagged twelve chicks. That's right, I said twelve. Okay, so I didn't really bag all of them myself. I have to admit that I had help. There were two other guys and a girl. But between the four of us we managed to get the job done.

Me? I bagged five or six chicks and then helped the others.

The thing is, these weren't just ordinary chicks. They were the kind Mom would approve of me bringing home … you know, cute, cuddly, and sweet, if not a little feathery.

We set out that evening from our sailboat, the *Copper Sky*, with a simple mission: we were to intercept any chicks that headed down to the beach and try to bag them. This had sounded like a pastime I often dreamed about, so I had volunteered.

Our "chick mission" had straightforward objectives: we were to listen for the chicks, shine our lights on them, corner them, grab them, bag them, and then beach them. No problem!

Did I mention that these chicks were only two days old, and that they were wearing an odd sort of black-and-white feathered bikini?

To be honest, I never thought crouching in the sand and waiting expectantly in the dark and cold for the sound of scampering birds could be so much fun. But it is, man, it is! In fact, I have rarely been as excited about anything in my life. Have I gone crazy? I don't think so, but I do know that I now have a newfound respect for seabird researchers. And I have a new favourite seabird, the tiny black-and-white ancient murrelet.

Tonight we took part in a study of seabirds on Limestone Island, just north of Gwaii Haanas National Park Reserve in the Queen Charlottes archipelago. It is a twenty-five-year study gathering long-term data on the ancient murrelet—factors that affect their nesting habits, the growth and decline of their population over time, and so on.

Our guide, Chris, was a murrelet researcher. He met our skiff in a serene lagoon at dusk on one side of the island, and then led us on a journey of seabird discovery along winding paths and through towering old-growth forests. We learned about the project and the researchers, their goals and objectives, the obstacles they had encountered, and their findings to date. As we toured their research camp, he pointed out ancient murrelet burrows and discussed the island's ecology with us.

And then, when it was really dark, we split into two teams of four people and sat patiently at the bottom of a ravine, listening for the first sounds of murrelet chicks scurrying past us along the forest floor.

My team was assigned to watch two "funnels," Funnel Three and Funnel Four, which were the lower ends of two ravines that came together to form a W shape. Our job, Chris explained, was to capture any murrelet chicks that appeared in these funnels, then place them in small bags and bring them over to the banding station. After each chick had been weighed and outfitted with a small metal leg band that would help the researchers identify it in the future, we were to take the chicks to the beach, point them toward the shore, and release them so that they could meet up with their parents in the ocean.

What had originally sounded simple was now beginning to look rather complicated.

First of all, it was pitch-black. Not just dark, but *completely* dark. I'm talking full-out, middle-of-the-night, see-nothing kind of dark. And we were supposed to sit at the bottom of these funnels in this absolute darkness and listen for ancient murrelet chicks scurrying toward us? What the heck does a murrelet chick sound like when it's scurrying? My team didn't have a clue. To make matters worse, the chicks were supposedly small, fast, and extremely slippery.

After a quick huddle, it became apparent that we weren't altogether confident in our skills. We couldn't see a thing and we were worried about crushing the chicks when we did capture them. In short, we had no idea what we were doing, and we were anxious to begin.

The team was patient for about five minutes. We heard several different noises, none of which sounded to any of us like an ancient murrelet chick coming our way. We had been well schooled by Chris before he let us loose on this important mission, but the tension was mounting. At 11:40, ten minutes after our shift had started, we moved impatiently over the trail from Funnel Three to Funnel Four. Still nothing.

Then, at about ten minutes past midnight, as we walked from Funnel Four back to Funnel Three, we rounded the corner and suddenly realized that there were chicks in our funnel. We immediately began to panic ... er, I mean, we calmly approached the chicks, caught them, and bagged them.

In reality, of course, we scrambled around like idiots, tripping over ourselves before we finally managed to turn our flashlights on. We suddenly spotted two tiny, egg-sized, black-and-white bundles of fuzz scampering back and forth against the plastic sheets that were set up at the edge of our funnel.

"Catch it! ... He's going left! ... No, right! Get him! ... Geez, they move fast! Bloody hell! ... Put it in the bag headfirst. NO! Headfirst, not by the legs! ... Ouch! ... Ahhhh!"

And that, my friends, is the sound of rookie murrelet-catchers calmly catching and bagging chicks for the very first time.

I should just say that the real researchers, assuming that the four of us were competent, had left us to catch and bag these birds on our own. Surprisingly enough, once we got over our initial excitement, we did manage to catch on. The whole process of catching and bagging our first two chicks, delivering them to the researchers for banding, and then releasing them onto the beach took twenty minutes. And by the time we returned to Funnel Three, there were two more chicks waiting for us.

That was pretty much how our evening went for the next ninety minutes. In total, our group caught twelve murrelet chicks and one adult (Chris thought the adult was trying to lead its chick down to the beach).

For my part, I still can't believe I had so much fun catching birds, but thanks to Chris and twelve little cuties, I left Limestone Island with a lot more than knowledge. I left with a newfound love for a little seabird, and a wild tale about the night I bagged twelve chicks.

When Canmore-based writer and photographer John Marriott isn't chasing chicks, he can be found chasing bears and other wild beasts from Yellowstone to the Yukon. You can view John's spectacular nature photography and read more of his tall tales online at www.wildernessprints.com.

Family Picnic

Sit, roll over, fetch ... good doggies!

By Linda Beaulieu

"Are we there yet? I'm hungry," I whined.

"Are we where? Do you think I can just make a picnic spot materialize out of thin air?" Mom asked.

It was hot and sweaty in the back seat of our red Pontiac station wagon, and the seats were a vinyl torture chamber. Mom tried to remedy this by spreading one of our unzipped sleeping bags across the back seat, which only added to the torture. Our poor limbs rubbed against the zipper-cum-branding iron in the sun. Three kids shoved into the back of a car with no air conditioning was as unbearable for us as it was for our parents.

I liked sitting in the middle because at least I could stretch out my legs through the front seat armrest. That made it easier to deal with my little brother on one side and my older sister on the other. My brother was five and I liked having someone younger than me around, even if he was the cute one now. My sister was older so she thought she was better than either of us. It was a chore for her to be around us.

"I can't stand it anymore!" my sister shrieked. "They're too close to me! I need some space!" The joys of another Chabassol family vacation were beginning to wear thin. We had been driving for seven hours already and it was only noon. We all hoped that a picnic lunch and a good stretch would make the next seven hours bearable. I never understood why we had to drive like maniacs. Why couldn't the vacation start when we left the house? Why did it have to wait until we reached our destination?

"I'm dying of thirst!" I pleaded with my parents, in case they had forgotten it was time for a break.

"Shut up, I am trying to listen to my music," my sister cried, poking me. "It's important that I know all the lyrics for the next club meeting. Na na na na, you got it girl, yeah!"

"By the sounds of it, they're quite the lyricists." Dad was trying to be funny again. He just couldn't understand my sister's obsession with the new rock band, Boyz R Us.

"You listen to old geezer music. You don't know anything," my sister retorted. "I'm hungry, too. When are we gonna stop and eat? It's hot in here and everyone keeps interrupting my music. I want to get out."

"I understand that," Mom said, trying to sound calm. "If everyone would stop yelling at each other and start looking for a picnic area, we would be able to get out of the car for a while."

I stared out the windshield, straight ahead for a few minutes. I liked to be able to see the rolling hills and mountains in the distance. It was almost like sitting in the front. Once we reached the mountains, the rest areas would multiply, with picnic areas every ten kilometres or so. Unfortunately, we weren't there yet and the pickings were slim.

Beside me, my little brother started to snore.

"Arghh! Make him stop," my sister complained. "I can't stand that sound his nose makes. It's disgusting! He sounds like a dying elephant. Make him stop or I'm jumping out the window."

"Promises, promises," Mom muttered under her breath.

My sister threw her Walkman at my brother, who woke up crying. I ducked and covered my head with a pillow, somewhat dulling the noise of my family erupting into chaos: my brother crying, Mom yelling, my sister whining and justifying her attitude (as Mom liked to say). The battle lines were drawn and with tensions high, this war could last a while. Peeking out from under the pillow, I could see Dad's white knuckles gripping the steering wheel, his face staring straight ahead.

I don't remember who spotted the sign first: REST AREA FIVE KM. It didn't matter at that point. We had not seen any sign of civilization in over forty-five minutes. It was about time. None of us was making a fuss any more. We even waited, silently, while Dad drove around the parking lot to find the spot with the most shade.

My brother was bouncing with excitement, no doubt thinking about the chocolate chip cookies for dessert. My sister was always anxious to be away from us for a while. What I liked best was how you breathed different air when you got out of the car. It smelled good. There were three or four families in the park but you could not tell who belonged to whom. We picked the nearest picnic table with a tree for some shade.

Dad brought out the cooler and we ate sandwiches, apples, and cookies, feeding our crusts to the birds. Mom opened her book and stretched out on the bench, leaving us to blow off some steam and fill our tummies. There were two dogs playing nearby, and I started throwing them bits of my bologna and mustard sandwich, bringing them closer to our table. They were big husky dogs, although one of them looked somewhat mangy and a bit smaller. Was he the sidekick? I loved dogs and tried to convince Mom and Dad that we should get one because all our friends had pets.

The dogs came closer, smelling our food. I liked the big one. He sat regally while I fed him a few pieces of bologna. The smaller one pushed his muzzle in and started snapping for his share. Mom said she didn't trust them, that they looked shifty. We ignored her; she was never very friendly to animals. My brother held up a pickle.

"Beg for it, doggy," he cooed.

"Be careful," Mom cautioned. "These are strange dogs, and we don't know if they're safe."

"Aww Mom, we're just playing." He tried to get them to do other tricks too, but they didn't know any, which was a shame because they looked like smart dogs. "Shake a paw," "sit," and "roll over" all ended with the dogs snapping the food out of my brother's hand as he called the commands. I was beginning to think that Mom was right and my brother might lose a finger, or maybe worse. Apparently Dad agreed.

"Listen to your mother," Dad snapped. "Anyone who has to use the bathroom better do so now, because we gotta get going."

"No way, those outhouses are rank!" whined my sister.

"Um, hey, did anyone notice that everyone else is gone?" I asked.

"They forgot their doggies," said my brother, sounding confused.

"Oh."

Mom and Dad looked at the dogs sniffing the table on either side of my brother. They looked at each other as one of the dogs growled and snatched at my brother's half-eaten sandwich.

"Get away from them!" Mom and Dad grabbed us and quickly started backing towards the car.

"Those aren't dogs, they're wolves!" Dad cried.

We climbed into the car, locked the doors, and stared out the window as Dad drove away.

Half an hour later, we let out a collective sigh. Then my brother said, "Hey we forgot the cooler, the rest of our food is in there."

Linda Beaulieu and her husband travel extensively in Saskatchewan, where they encounter a wide variety of wildlife with which they rarely share their lunch. She currently resides in Kindersley.

Runaway Couch

Living room furniture is on the loose in Canada's Maritimes.

By Brent Curry

RCMP Constable Kevin Demeau was diplomatic. He readily conceded that he wasn't sure how things worked where we came from.

Still, after spotting my Norwegian cycling partner and me pedalling in the opposite direction down a scenic stretch of coastal highway, a sense of duty had compelled him to turn back and fill us in on how things worked in rural New Brunswick. A quick chirp of his siren and flash of lights had brought us together by the roadside.

As storm clouds loomed overhead, he and his partner surveyed our bicycle. Ours was a lot like other tandem bikes one might spot on the road from time to time. It had two sets of pedals and very long lengths of chain. The frame was welded together and made of light but strong chromoly steel tubing. What made our bike so special, however—which is also what seemed to be Constable Demeau's chief concern—was the couch. It was an old leatherette loveseat. Our frame was built around it, and Eivind and I were perched on top of it. We sat side by side on the cushions, our legs extended in front of us to spin the pedals. I steered the bike with a tiller linked to the two front wheels on either side of the couch.

While Constable Demeau couldn't cite any specific laws or regulations concerning wheeled furniture, he put together some pretty solid arguments against our chosen means of travel. Much of the trouble had to do with the width of our contraption. At nearly two metres across, it was eight centimetres wider than a Lincoln Navigator. This alone may not have been such a problem had it not also been for our speed, which could have generously been described as pokey. And then there was the question of whether or not it qualified as a bicycle at all. If it did, then we were in violation of New Brunswick's helmet law.

Yet, despite all of our transgressions, Constable Demeau seemed at odds with himself over how to handle us. Though our couchbike may have posed an imminent threat to public safety, he had to admit that it was indeed "a nice rig." He said that it might be against his better judgment, but he was going to let us go. "Do whatever you guys think is best," he said. We assured him we would keep an eye on traffic and pull off into the ditch whenever cars came by.

While the law had been merciful with us, the weather was not so kind. Minutes after the RCMP cruiser pulled away, the rain started coming down in buckets. We scrambled to cover the couch with our form-fitting tarp. Although it protected the precious faux leather fabric, it did nothing for the two of us. In fact, because we were sitting on top of the tarp, the water just pooled in the depressions where our wet bodies sank into the cushions, creating a sort of mobile Mr. Turtle pool.

The rain didn't let up all day. I started feeling guilty about what I was subjecting my innocent friend to. However, if he had any grievances about our state of affairs—his drenched cotton underwear, the erratic way I drove the couch off the steep edge of the road each time a car came by—he certainly wasn't letting on. He seemed to be content in the face of it all.

Surely anyone else would have been ruing the day they'd agreed to join me on this bizarre adventure. In Eivind's case, if he'd wanted to roll back time and extract himself from this soggy torment, the pivotal moment would have been several months earlier.

*　　　*　　　*

Through the magic of the Internet, Eivind had tracked me down to say hello. It had been over a decade since he'd been to Canada for a high school exchange and we'd been out of touch ever since. He was planning to come back on vacation and wanted to hook up with some old friends for a trip. Little did he know what he was getting himself into.

For me, past adventures had generally entailed epic feats of endurance, often coupled with severe physical discomfort. Never before had I done a trip based purely on whimsy. But what I had in mind this time was different, and for some reason Eivind struck me as an ideal partner in crime. Perhaps this was because English was his second language and he wouldn't readily question the odd juxtaposition of words like "ninety-five-pound chesterfield" with such terms as "self-contained bicycle travel."

Ultimately, it probably had more to do with Eivind's easygoing nature and his willingness to try all things new than it did with my sly tactics. Nevertheless, within a couple of days he sent back his response. I had myself a Norwegian crew member.

*   *   *

Over the following weeks, I proceeded to obtain a massive heap of steel tubing and aluminum billet. I began cutting it up and welding it into form. Eivind would drop me a line every now and then just to find out how I was getting along. I couldn't lie. Having no appreciable time management skills, I was finding it tough to make any headway against such worthy adversaries as work and television. I always assured him that despite being behind schedule, I was confident we'd be ready to roll when he arrived.

When Eivind finally arrived at the end of July, my cheeks were stuffed like a hamster's from all the words I'd been eating. Our couchbike wasn't anywhere near ready to roll. On the way home from the airport, I couldn't tell Eivind what the next few weeks would have in store for us. I had no idea whether another couple of day's work would yield the most fantastic touring bicycle known to man, or a feckless monstrosity I'd need to borrow a farmer's tractor to drag off my property. With no idea what kind of performance to expect, we could only speak in vague terms about a cycling route. We both agreed that the Maritimes sounded nice.

It was a good thing that over the next few days Eivind had some other friends he wanted to visit. And when he wasn't doing that, I had the benefit of what one of my housemates had started calling "cheap Norwegian sweatshop labour." After three days of round-the-clock toil in the sweltering heat of my garage, our joint venture of nations was finally complete. We rode it proudly around the block, and then, because we hadn't eaten a square meal since Eivind arrived, we rode it to the local grocery store to buy food for a celebratory dinner.

Leaving the grocery store, we didn't have any trouble locating our vehicle among the rows of parked cars. Ours was the one with the crowd around it. As we would realize more and more in the coming weeks, everyone had a different reaction to our couchbike. In this instance, the group of mostly older ladies was downright earnest in their praise for the comfortable-looking design. Furthermore, they were obviously embarrassed to have let one of the hottest youth trends slip past their pop culture radar; they sheepishly admitted this was the first bike of the sort they had seen. When we left them, I could only wonder how much longer they stood there waiting for the next pair of youngsters to come cruising by, looking for a spot to park their living room furniture.

All told, we only logged about three kilometres of testing the couchbike, but time being of the essence, we decided to leave the next day. So we tore down the bike, primed and painted it, and the next morning headed off in a roughly eastward direction.

There was no fanfare to greet us when we arrived at our arbitrarily selected starting point in Miramichi, New Brunswick.

There were no marching bands, clashing cymbals, or beating drums as we extracted piece after piece of our couchbike from the impossibly small van and laid them out for assembly in the parking lot. There was no horn section responding in crescendo as wheels were mounted and cushions were put in place. And there wasn't anyone lurking in the bushes with lips pursed against a giant tuba. It's a shame about the tuba player, because that musician would surely have had his moment. At the height of all the frenzy, the tuba man could have blown an abrupt and dissonant tone to silence the band as I came to the realization that a critical component of our couchbike had been left behind. In any event, there I was—immersed in silence, pale-faced and sweaty-palmed, trying to explain the predicament to Eivind.

Without getting overly technical, the crux of the situation was this: I had built a custom clamp to lock down the bearings of our steering mechanism and permit precise tensioning of these bearings by way of a tuning bolt. Although I had left this critical component behind, all was not lost. It was with great relief, I realized, that we still had the wherewithal to clamp the bearings. Unfortunately, the precision adjustment would have to be achieved by walloping the bearings with a rubber mallet, a tactic we executed with mediocre but satisfactory results.

Within a few hours we'd reassembled our bike and cautiously began our journey along the wide shoulder of Highway 11. After about seven kilometres, we turned down a small side road in search of the coastal highway. We were taking up a full lane as there was no shoulder, but we were cruising along, and the light traffic flowed around us in a procession of cars and trucks occupied by people in hysterical fits of laughter. Many were so tickled to see a couch rolling down the road that they dangled out their windows to take pictures of the spectacle.

Brent and Eivind (right) navigate their couchbike the length of Prince Edward Island.

Eivind was sitting shotgun and had the map spread open in front of him looking for our turn. The turn came quicker than we expected. Although I had access to brakes for both sides of the bike, excitement got the better of me and I squeezed only the left brake lever—the one that was mounted on the tiller. This threw our equilibrium off kilter and the couch went into a high-speed wobble. Suddenly, one of the wheels swung too far and jammed against the side of the couch. It happened in an instant but it felt like slow motion. I felt the couch lift up beneath me. I watched as Eivind was launched into the air, pitching head-first over the pedals. At the pinnacle of our trajectory everything seemed to be balanced precariously on the two front wheels. Then, slowly, everything came crashing back down. The luggage, which had been mounted behind the couch, landed on top of the bike. The couch came down on top of the luggage. Once the dust had settled, and I was still clinging to the couch, I looked down to discover I was sitting about a metre higher than before.

Eivind picked himself off the highway. I was glad he wasn't hurt. Together, we began clearing the wreckage from the road. We lifted the couch into the ditch and pitched all the bags on top of it. When we went to move the bike itself, I noticed one of the wheels was no longer touching the ground. We moved it across the intersection to a dead-end lane for closer inspection. Even standing on the frame with all my weight, and jumping up and down to flex the rear suspension, I couldn't bring the fourth wheel back into contact with the ground. I feared the frame had become irreparably mangled. Then, after studying it for several minutes, I realized the telescoping tubes of the frame had simply twisted inside one another. All we had to do was loosen the pinch bolts and straighten everything out.

As I began tightening the bolts on the frame, a pickup truck pulled up and the driver leaned out the window.

"You know what I'm going to ask," he said. "What the heck is that?"

Eivind responded casually by stating it was a bike.

"Where do you sit?" was the next question.

"On a couch," replied Eivind.

"On a what?"

Eivind pointed across the intersection at the large piece of furniture resting by the roadside. "On a couch," he said again.

A period of stunned silence followed. This would prove to be a typical encounter. From there, more questions were asked. The central theme tended to be "Why?" This was a line of questioning to which we could never offer a completely satisfactory answer. But as long as people were smiling and laughing, we knew we were on the same wavelength and that's all we could really hope for.

As we finished torquing the last bolt in our couchbike frame, a police car turned up the road and stopped for a moment by our stack of cargo. Through his rear window I could see his head shaking as though refusing to believe his eyes. The officer drove off without any closer inspection.

We hit the road again. As the day wore on, we regained our confidence and were enjoying the simultaneous experience of physical activity and relaxed lounging. It made moot the argument to "get off the couch and do something." More to the point, the maritime scenery was beautiful and people in the passing motorhomes were as much a source of amusement for us as we seemed to be for them.

Nearing the town of Baie-Sainte-Anne, we were just beginning to look for a place to camp when a police cruiser pulled up beside us. He rolled down his passenger side window and in a resigned tone said, "I don't want to be a stickler but I don't think that thing's legal. And if that's a bicycle, you guys should have helmets on." Yes, yes—the helmet issue. That was something we had debated at length before our departure. Our two main questions had seemed to answer themselves: "How fast are we ever really going to be travelling on a 95-pound couch?" and "Isn't there already sufficient padding on this thing anyway?"

Of course, after Eivind had been launched into flight from our unassuming couch, the flaws in our logic had been made abundantly clear. We assured the police officer we would be purchasing helmets in the next town. With that, he pulled away and was gone.

Two days later, we woke to pouring rain. We were further down the coast of New Brunswick but still hadn't found anywhere to buy helmets. The day before, we'd had our run-in with Constable Demeau, and ever since, our bike had been taking quite a beating from all the driving on and off the road in our futile attempts to be unobtrusive to motorists.

We needed to give one of the wheels a good tuning. But alas, on top of everything else that had happened, our tools had been stolen the night before. With so much conspiring against us, we decided to reorganize and drive to Prince Edward Island. Hitchhiking back to the van proved to be a great decision. After a day of errands and driving, we'd acquired helmets, repaired our wheel, and lugged our couch across the Confederation Bridge to the quaint sanctuary of PEI.

The next day we reassembled the couchbike near the town of Tignish. Tignish is located at the northwestern end of the Confederation Trail, a multi-use pathway built over an abandoned rail line. Over the next few days we would follow this trail eastward.

But first, we wanted to ride west to the coast. We relished the thought of not only travelling the full length of the trail, but also crossing the island from tip to tip. This would surely be a first for human-powered couch travel.

Our outing to the coast was a terrific ride. We made it back to Tignish just in time to attend the blueberry social at the community centre. While trying not to eat more than our share of home-baked desserts, we watched a cast of young and old belt out a fine medley of songs.

The next day, as we rode east along the hard-packed gravel trail, Eivind and I discovered we both had the same song in our heads. It was a George Jones tune that a young boy had performed the night before. It was called "Choices" and the words seemed to speak to me:

> *I've had choices since the day I was born.*
> *There were voices that told me right from wrong.*
> *If I had listened,*
> *No I wouldn't be here today living and dying*
> *With the choices I've made.*

Right or wrong, good or bad, it was definitely a string of my own strange choices that had brought me to pedal through PEI's pastoral setting on a fake leather couch. Given the perfect sunny weather, I wouldn't say these were choices I altogether regretted.

Meanwhile, Eivind was singing his own version of the song, though he couldn't quite work out the lyrics. He didn't realize it was about choices. He thought it had something to do with horses.

That the song lyrics had registered so spuriously in his Norwegian ears was a reminder of Eivind's innocence in this affair. But whether he lamented his choices or cared more about a secret passion for horses, one thing was clear: I had a kindred spirit in Eivind. Who else would have endured the hassles of pedalling a chesterfield across PEI?

While the Confederation Trail provided a welcome respite from traffic, that freedom came at a tremendous cost. The Confederation Trail regularly criss-crosses roads and highways. At each crossing, barricades have been erected to keep cars and trucks from accessing the trail. A narrow gap remains open for pedestrians and cyclists to squeeze through. Unfortunately, the visionaries that established this wonderful corridor never accounted for what some cyclists would be lugging along with them. As a result, upwards of twenty times a day we would engage in the task of dismantling our bicycle, lifting it over the barricade, carrying it across the road, and reassembling it on the other side of the second barricade. We got to be pretty efficient at this. Occasionally we would time ourselves. After we got good at it, five minutes was typical.

Wherever possible, we would strive to avoid these dreaded portages. Sometimes it was simple; we could just ride up onto a grassy lawn and skirt the gate. Other times proved to be more difficult. A trench or a small bush might cause us to stop and weigh our options. Unseen swamps and thorns would often make us regret our cavalier ways.

As we forged across the island, we won the respect and sympathy of many for all the hardships we were enduring. People spoke as though this expedition by couch represented one of the more significant historical crossings of the small island province. One local cyclist told us about the National Boy Scout Jamboree of 2001 and how all the trail gates had been opened for the associated bicycle tour. He insisted that we deserved the same concessions. "What you two are doing is far more important than any National Boy Scout Jamboree!" he declared. We were flattered by this exaggerated comparison.

Before riding off, he passed on a few phone numbers of people he thought could help us track down a master key for all the gates. We gave them a try but the effort proved fruitless.

So we soldiered on. Along the way we were interviewed by local papers, we were offered places to stay for the night, and we were served cold drinks. We even ventured down a branch trail to Charlottetown. But as enamoured as we were with the Confederation Trail, as we neared the end of the track in Elmira, we found the gravel becoming intolerably soft and loose. Our speed had dwindled to no more than a brisk walking pace. We had been tempted many times before, but we finally decided to bid farewell to the trail and head for the coast by road.

While both the dirt and paved road surfaces were immeasurably faster than the gravel path, the steep, long hills of eastern PEI provided their own unique challenges, both in the ascents and the descents. Although the couchbike had two independent drive trains, each with 144 different gear combinations, the gear ratios were disproportionately skewed toward the high range. While our high gear was more than double that of a standard mountain bike, our low gear was only seven-per cent lower than normal. So we struggled and sometimes had to push our bike up the hills. Rolling down the opposite sides, we were never brave or crazy enough to let the couchbike reach its maximum speed. Once, we let the speedometer creep up to forty-four kilometres an hour, but a palpable fear of death persuaded me to put the brakes on before we went any faster.

Another time, on a dirt road, I was too afraid to apply the brakes. I should never have let us get going that fast to begin with, but we had reached the point of no return. Because of the inconsistent dirt surface, I feared that braking hard could cause us to spin out of control. As the couch hurtled closer and closer toward terminal velocity, all noise became muted. I can still hear Eivind's last words: "I'm scared."

"Don't be scared," I replied with a calmness belied by my posture on the couch. I had assumed a sort of starfish stance on the cushions, my legs and arms spread wide in preparation for a crash landing. And that's when our worst fears were realized. One wheel jammed and the couch spun into a huge doughnut. The world swirled around us. Strangely, I felt very calm. This was one smooth doughnut.

When we finally came to rest, I couldn't recall how many rotations we'd made, but the couchbike was pointing uphill. Mechanically, everything was perfectly fine. I couldn't believe our luck. Giddy from the adrenaline, we laughed hysterically at our good fortune.

Later that day, as we left the town of Souris bound for the easternmost tip of Prince Edward Island, a police car passed us and immediately pulled into a nearby parking lot. This elicited our primal flight instincts. We were still feeling like outlaws from our earlier dealings with the police. As the officer got out of his car and went fishing for something in his trunk, Eivind and I plotted our damage control strategy. The officer started walking toward us; there was obviously no escaping this confrontation.

I think the ensuing exchange caught all parties off guard. It turned out the friendly police officer wanted nothing more than to introduce himself and to take a picture to show the wife and kids. He even asked if we were raising money for something. He seemed quite prepared to contribute to our cause. Meanwhile, our nerves were so rattled we were barely able to break out of a "yes sir," "no sir" line of response. At least our smiles in parting were expressive and heartfelt.

We would wear those smiles through the day and straight through to the next morning, when we rolled up to the lighthouse at East Point, Prince Edward Island. Our odyssey complete, we gazed with satisfaction over the steep sandstone cliffs to the ocean below.

Today, the couch sits quietly in my living room at home. No medals or ceremonial afghans adorn its backrest. But every so often, in a search for the television remote, cushions will be overturned to reveal some small treasure like a seashell or a stone. These, and the memories they evoke, are life's true treasures.

Brent Curry is the president and CEO of the Bicycle Forest— a place where no object is safe from being mounted with wheels and pedals, and where all the furniture has a secret past. You can visit the Bicycle Forest on the web at www.bikeforest.com.

The Marmots of Mongolia

They're small, cute, furry, and not altogether pleasant.

By Clemens Schneider

The sun was already high in the sky when my brother Simon and I found the market. There was only one small problem—it was completely deserted.

This was not what we had expected. Mongolian markets, like markets in many countries, are an exercise in pandemonium—vendors hawking goat's milk, leather-skinned men laughing and tugging at mugs of *süütei tsai* (salty tea), sheep frolicking and defecating in the streets.

But the village that morning had an abandoned feel to it. The sun was piercing; the wind whistled along dirt streets like the word "sarsaparilla" escaping from between a cowboy's missing front teeth. We half expected to see tumbleweeds whirling past us, to hear eerie, warbling harmonica music, to see a desperado with an oily handlebar moustache named Bad Bart pull up on his braying steed, draw his pistol, and start firing at us.

But there was no Bad Bart, no tumbleweeds, and no harmonica music to greet us. There was nothing but silence.

We were in Mongolia to hike for a few days through the arid steppe country at the edge of the Gobi Desert. I had been working with street children in Ulaanbaatar for several weeks, and the remote Mongolian hills had been beckoning. When my brother Simon arrived, we hopped on board an old Russian truck and travelled to the remote village of Zezerleg, navigating miles of potholed gravel roads ("roads" is used here in the loosest possible manner) from Karakorum.

Before leaving on our hike, of course, we had to purchase food, which left us in a bit of a dilemma. So we wandered through Zezerleg's narrow streets, searching for any sign of life. We finally passed a large, concrete building that looked rather official, like some sort of government building. A mob of more than a hundred people was assembled outside—yelling and screaming and jostling for position—waving passports above their heads. Although it confirmed that people actually live in Zezerleg, it offered no explanation as to why the market was closed.

We finally stumbled across a small vendor where we were able to purchase several days worth of food. We stocked up on bread, sausage, chocolate, and several cans of tuna fish. The small, skinny Mongolian lady behind the counter smiled kindly at us and graciously took our Tukreks. For five days of food, we paid the equivalent of thirty US dollars.

As we walked toward the edge of town, however, we noticed for the first time a police car and several officers blocking the road. "Let's try walking past them first," I suggested to my brother. "If they try to stop us, just pretend you don't understand what they're saying."

As we approached the blockade, two police officers stepped forward and held up their hands. A casual amble through the blockade was obviously not going to work. The officer on the right wore a grave expression on his face, while the officer on the left spoke fast and furiously in his native tongue, no doubt explaining local protocol.

"But we only want to go hiking!" I pleaded. "We're not planning to camp anywhere near your town." I recognized a few Mongolian words from my two months spent in Ulaanbaatar, but the policemen were talking too quickly. I really had no idea what they were saying. The only thing obvious was that we were going nowhere.

When the officer stopped talking, I again tried to explain that we were innocent foreigners who merely wanted to go hiking for a few days. We didn't want to poach any sheep. We wouldn't abduct any Mongolian girls. Indeed, Germans were actually quite nice. I tried to mime hiking through the hills, hoping they would understand and let us pass. But it was useless. The policemen appeared genuinely sorry for having to stop us, but they would still have nothing to do with our hiking plans.

After several fruitless minutes of pleading and miming, miming and pleading, a woman in her middle years approached us. She had black hair and weather-beaten skin. She was wearing a *del*, the typical dress of all Mongolians, a long robe made of silk that protects against the cold wind. The lady said something to the officers, lifted up her arms as though she were holding a rifle, and then mock fired over the hills. Is this what would happen to us if we tried to escape?

Simon looked at me with a worried expression, but I remained calm. Maybe they were trying to explain something—something about guns or hunting—so I asked the woman, but of course she couldn't understand German or English. Then I remembered the small English-Mongolian dictionary in my backpack. I unzipped the top pouch, pulled it out, and started paging through, looking for the word "hunter."

When I found the word, I tried pronouncing it, and the woman nodded encouragingly. Then she pulled her hands in close to her chest and stuck her front teeth over her bottom lip. What was she trying to say now? She looked like a squirrel begging for peanuts.

A rodent ... of course ... a rodent. On the way to Zezerleg, we had seen hunters driving around with dead marmots in their trucks. Hurriedly, I paged through my dictionary until I found the Mongolian word for "marmot."

The woman grew excited when I spat out the word, and despite butchering it, my discovery caught the attention of the police officers, too. They smiled and nodded at one another, and looked appreciatively towards us. Maybe we weren't so dumb after all.

Suddenly, I felt my throat tighten. I could feel tiny beads of sweat forming along my brow. I looked down at my brother, who had some minutes ago handed responsibility for negotiations over to me and was now sitting casually at the roadside rolling a cigarette. I paged slowly through the dictionary looking for a word I hoped I wouldn't find, but knew was there. I took a deep breath and spat it out.

The woman was plainly ecstatic. She reached over and gave me a big hug as the police officers erupted in public celebration. It was like I was a contestant on *The Price is Right*, and had just won the Sports Car and the Dream Home in the bonus round. I was *The Man*. The police officers danced around their car, laying high fives on each other.

"Way to go Clemens," my brother enthused, rising from his perch. "You figured it out. So what's going on?"

I could only manage a feeble smile. "I looked up the word plague," I told him. "It appears this town is under quarantine because of an outbreak of the black plague."

Simon's face suddenly went white.

"I remember hearing about it from a guy in Ulaanbaatar," I continued. "Some of the marmots in Mongolia carry fleas that transmit the disease."

The police officers were still dancing jubilantly in the middle of the street, so I interrupted them. "How long is the quarantine?" I asked in German, and then paged through my dictionary to figure out the translation. It was a slow and painful process.

One of the police officers finally understood and waved his hand in the air as though we had nothing to worry about. After a great deal of gesturing and creative sign language, we were able to determine that it wouldn't be long. The man held up three, then four fingers.

"Well, three or four hours isn't too long," said Simon with a sigh of relief.

"I think he means days," I corrected. I paged through my little dictionary until I found the word for "day," but the officer shook his head.

"You mean three or four weeks?" I stammered. I looked up the word for "week" and sure enough, that was the time frame they were referring to.

"But my plane leaves for Europe in a few days!" protested Simon.

"And I have to work next week," I said. "But I don't think these guys care. C'mon, let's go back into the village and figure things out." Of course, Lonely Planet had no advice whatsoever about what to do should you get inadvertently exposed to the black plague.

After discussing the situation, I must admit that we decided to attempt escape. Even though there were only three roads entering and exiting the village (all of which were blockaded), the logistics of getting out were really not that difficult. It would be easy enough to hike up to the top of one of the hills bordering the village and then drop down into the next valley. Once out of the village we would hike for several days over the hill country until we crossed a road. Then we would hitchhike.

We bought several litres of bottled water because we weren't sure if the local water was safe to drink, and then studied the surrounding hills for a likely place to make our escape. The Mongolian Steppe is treeless, which meant we would be easy to spot. We suspected that all of the men in the village owned guns, which was clearly a downside to our plan. But the thought of being stranded in a remote Mongolian village under black plague quarantine, I suppose, scared us more than gunshot wounds. So it was escape or bust.

Luckily everything went strictly to plan, and it wasn't fifteen minutes before we reached the crest of the large hill and gingerly tiptoed down the far side. Not a single warning shot was fired.

That's when we saw something that looked like an astronaut walking towards us. It was descending a hill to the east, wearing a plastic suit and gas mask. We didn't know what to do. Fortunately, the astronaut walked past us without so much as a gesture, and we continued on our way.

It was another three or four hours of hiking before we came to our first group of yurts. Mongolians are by nature and tradition nomadic people, and many of them still hunt while travelling in caravans—these days by truck or horse. Yurts are the high-tech tents that nomads live in. They are round, cylinder-shaped on top, and can be constructed and taken down with ease. All of the walls and rafters tension against each other, so there is no need for ropes to hold them in place, and they are practically indestructible, even when blasted by the high winds of the Steppe.

The nomads greeted us warmly. One of the men saw that I had a guitar slung over my shoulder, and before long he and a group of his comrades were insisting I play a few songs. I couldn't really say no, considering the great karma deficit we now faced after escaping from Zezerleg. So I pulled out my guitar and started to strum.

We all sat down around the yurt's fire pit as I plucked a few strings, wondering what to play. The nomads smiled expectantly at me, their mystery guitar man. "All right," I finally said. "This is a song from my homeland. It's called *Wir Lagen von Madagascar*."

My brother's eyes bulged like saucers and after one verse he started laughing hysterically, the stress of the day washing away in a great flood of emotion. The nomads clearly loved it, too.

For my part, I sang the song without pausing for breath. It had to be that way. The song was about a ship of German sailors who got stuck off the coast of Madagascar, no wind to move their ship, until one of the men caught the black plague and eventually died. We were just grateful the Mongolian Steppe is a very windy place.

Clemens Schneider has travelled around the world several times. He recently returned to Germany where he happily lives plague free.

Up the Creek

I am little mountain stream, hear me roar!

By Darren Arsenault

I awoke with a start to the sound of Herb's voice shouting across the campsite. Sitting up in the dark, I groped for my watch. It was 4:30 A.M. What could he possibly be yelling about at this time of night? The rain was beating a steady cadence on the roof of the trailer, drowning out a faint rushing sound that I was still too groggy to place. I shook my head to clear it and then Herb's voice came again.

"Darren, wake up!"

The urgency in his voice was like a slap in the face. Jumping up from bed, I hurried to the door. The rushing noise now filled me with a sense of dread. My fears were confirmed at the sight of the roiling brown liquid confronting me outside my door. Wavelets of water were kissing the top step of my tent trailer. Less than eight hours before, this same step had been a metre above dry ground. The little creek we had camped beside was now a murky, swollen river. Stepping into the current, Herb and I quickly assessed the situation.

"Let's get the hell out of here!" I said.

"What about the trailers?"

"Forget 'em! They're not worth drowning over."

Herb managed to get his family inside his truck while I woke my wife and kids. There was a large tree beside the bridge that had led us to this idyllic site, and—across the bridge—the gravel road that would lead us to safety. I was very grateful for the tree because it acted as a marker. Herb rumbled through the water; staying left of the tree as he crossed the bridge ensured that he wouldn't drive his truck into the creek bed.

It didn't take long to rouse Dawn and the kids, and we were soon wading toward my truck as fast as we could move. As we approached, I could see that it was tilted at an odd angle. A bloody flat tire! Great! Changing flats is no fun at the best of times, but you haven't been challenged until you try it in a metre of water. I must work well under pressure because I changed the tire in Guinness-record time. We quickly drove across the bridge, and although wet and miserable, we were safe.

*   *   *

What better way to end nearly two weeks of camping than with a pre-dawn flash flood! We had left Red Deer, Alberta on the Canada Day weekend for the only two weeks of vacation I would have all year. I was pulling a collapsible tent trailer, and travelling with my wife Dawn; our eleven-year-old, Angela; our five-year-old, Anthony; and our dog Nikita. Our friends Herb and Shelley were pulling a regular trailer and had brought their son Lindsey, also eleven, and their cat.

We were all eager to camp at one of our favourite sites in the foothills, just outside of Nordegg, Alberta, where we had been going for many years. To get there, we had to drive a gravel road through a mixed forest of mostly spruce, pine, and poplar. After crossing a bridge, we immediately pulled off into a little clearing beside what looked like a perfect fly-fishing creek. By driving a little further off road and downstream, we arrived at a scenic spot just right for our trailers. We enjoyed the area for many reasons. First, it wasn't in a campground, so it was free. Second, it was beside a tumbling creek, about three metres wide. Third, it was free. Fourth, it offered ample opportunities for fishing, hiking, and playing in the sun. Fifth, it was free. Needless to say, it was a great spot to relax, soak up nature, and have a great time with old friends.

The first two days brought beautiful weather. We settled in, relaxed, and enjoyed each other's company. I could feel the stress ooze from my fingertips. Then it started to rain. If it had rained solidly, we could have left with a clear conscience, knowing that staying would be useless. Unfortunately, the weather was a tease. The rain sprinkled, drizzled, and occasionally poured for ten straight days, but as soon as we started talking about leaving, it always let up enough to give us hope. So we stayed. After all, who would leave such an idyllic spot with the promise of better weather tomorrow?

On the tenth day of rain we finally gave up. Our plan was to pack up the next morning and return to Red Deer, giving us a couple of days to dry out and relax before I returned to the pressure-cooker of work. However, we had noticed a slight rise in the creek's water level, so I decided to put my mathematical skills to the test. I wanted to check just how quickly it was rising. After much figuring, I determined the water was rising about one-and-a-half centimetres every hour. And the creek bank was forty-six centimetres. It seemed logical, then, that we would be fine for the next thirty-six hours.

At four-thirty that morning, Herb's voice alerted me to the fact that either my logic was flawed or my Grade Four math skills were very rusty. Herb's trailer sat a little lower to the ground than mine, and he had been wakened by the sound of floodwaters lapping at his floorboards. Upstream dams had apparently started releasing excess water to avoid permanent damage, which was why the river had jumped its banks so quickly and was flowing directly into our campsite from upstream. Since we were camped on the low side of the drainage, we ended up in the middle of a very pissed-off river.

*   *   *

By five that morning, we had all made it to higher ground on the far side of the bridge. Across the bridge sat our two trailers and the bulk of our camping gear. The deluge had swallowed most of it, and I was certain that at least some of it was already ruined or floating downstream. The picture ahead wasn't much better. Brackish water had washed out the road downstream, which meant that we were effectively trapped on an island with rushing water in every direction. There was no way out.

It wasn't long before other campers began appearing from the bushes, until four or five groups had joined us. We decided the road underneath the water was not safe enough to try driving on, as it ran too close to the stream bank. If we misjudged the road's position, we could end up in much deeper water. It was apparent that the other campers were coming to the same conclusion, so we settled in for a long stay.

Now, seven people and two pets living in two small trucks would probably have raised the region's murder rate considerably, so Herb and I decided to pull our trailers across the bridge. We figured that it was better to hunker down with some semblance of comfort.

Deciding to retrieve the trailers and actually getting them, of course, proved to be two different matters. They were now immersed in a metre of fast flowing water. Working together for safety, we hooked Herb's trailer to his truck, hopped in and tried dragging it to safety. What had taken us a couple of hours to rig together took him seconds to pull across the bridge. A bit overeager, he pulled it across so fast that he badly scraped the side of the trailer on the marker tree.

My trailer was next, although initially it seemed to be stuck. Assuming I was just bogged down in the mud, I gunned the engine, which made the situation even worse. The wires under the trailer were caught on built-up debris, and as I accelerated forward, they ripped apart. These wires were necessary to raise the tent and I soon discovered that I could no longer set it up. First the flat tire and now this!

By this time we were all starved, so we piled into Herb's trailer for a late breakfast. Four adults, three kids, and two pets—all of us looking like drowned rats—made for an interesting meal. But we were all grateful for a little food and rest. We could count our blessings that we were alive, in no immediate danger, and had enough gear to be reasonably comfortable. We still had food and water and we were on dry ground.

About an hour later a park ranger appeared on the far side of the river. He instructed all the campers to go back across the bridge to where a helicopter would be able to land and rescue us. Although the bridge looked a little unsteady by this time, we followed his instructions. After getting across, we sat in our trucks and waited. About half an hour later the ranger returned to tell us the chopper wasn't coming after all. Apparently there were people in even more desperate trouble than we were. We were instructed to wait things out, and he would get back to us with a new rescue plan. We crossed back to the other side—a good thing because shortly thereafter we heard a terrible groan. A few seconds later the bridge was ripped from its moorings and washed downriver.

By this time I was feeling very frustrated, so I decided to risk driving my truck across the river. I had a big four-wheel drive Jeep, and I had driven the road many times before. I reasoned that I would be fine if I just took my time. Best of all, the others would be able to follow me. The kids wanted to come, so I loaded them and the dog into the truck and set off. Dawn stayed behind to salvage what she could and would follow with the others.

I drove very carefully to avoid the edge of the road. About halfway across, disaster struck: I misjudged the side of the road and began to slip down the creek bank. To make matters worse, a surge of churning water from upriver slammed some logs and drifting debris into the side of my truck and pushed us over the edge.

Immediately, the truck began to fill with water. I was in full panic mode, though we managed to climb into the truck bed through the rear window. I was in the middle of a raging river with my dog and two kids, and the island was at least a hundred metres away. The situation looked grim. I figured Nikita could swim to safety and I probably could too, but there was no way my kids would make it. Fortunately, Herb was still thinking clearly. He launched his little aluminum boat and brought us back to safety.

*   *   *

After a day and a half of waiting, all the campers were getting a little desperate. We didn't have much food left and cabin fever was starting to set in. Herb and I were considering how we might trap and kill a deer with our bare hands. The river wasn't rising anymore, but it hadn't started to drop either. And we still hadn't heard from the park ranger. For all we knew, we had been forgotten.

One of the other campers, a fellow with a huge four-by-four, finally got brave. Using my half-sunken truck as a marker and driving very slowly and carefully, he managed to make it across the roiling river. The rest of us soon followed, and all the stranded campers drove out in a convoy to safety. To this day, I like to think that without my strategically placed truck to mark the edge of the road, we might never have gotten out.

*   *   *

Red Deer never looked so good to my family and me. We dried off and cleaned up, and when we turned on the television, we were surprised to find ourselves on the national news. It's great to be famous, though I'm still waiting for the movie deals to roll in.

Three weeks later, the water levels had dropped enough for me to get my truck back. Using a winch and a well-positioned tree, we pulled it out of the river, dripping with mud and slime. I drove it into downtown Nordegg where it became locally famous. My slimy truck was the talk of the town for weeks. It's still waiting for a movie deal, too.

About two months later, my family drove back to see what had changed. Our campsite looked like a beach; the floodwaters had generously coated it with layers of sand and silt from upstream. Future unsuspecting campers can now enjoy a beach beside the quiet, burbling creek.

As for the bridge, it was completely ruined. The girders were twisted and chunks of concrete were falling off. The only trace of our belongings was a solitary lawn chair buried upside down in the sand, a fraction of its aluminum legs visible.

What lesson have I learned? Always check the names of natural features near campsites. We had camped beside a creek without knowing its name and suffered a stiff penalty as a result. For you see, after getting back to Red Deer, we discovered the name of the creek that gave us so much trouble: Lookout Creek … as in, "Lookout! The creek's about to kick our backsides!"

Darren Arsenault still lives in Red Deer, a city that is blessed with one of Canada's driest climates. He sells real estate by day and auditions for acting roles by night. Most recently, he played a cowboy on the Disney Channel's recreation of Little House on the Prairie.

Ice Cowboys

*How to survive the most gruelling winter race
in Canada.*

By Matt Jackson

The day that I first meet Barney McIlhargey, it is one of those
sublimely sunny Alberta mornings when it hardly feels like
winter at all. Yet it *is* winter, no question about it—the second
week in January, to be precise. The streets are clear of snow, the
birds are twittering contentedly from treetops, and the sunshine
feels almost balmy.

Mother Nature is either very confused or enjoying a practical
joke at the expense of Calgary's proud winter warriors: the ice
canoeists, or *Canotiers de Glace* as they're known in the largely
non-existent French circles on this side of the country.

Even the Bow River, which meanders past apartment
buildings and skyscrapers near downtown Calgary, is showing
only the faintest glimmer of a seasonal shift. Although there are
some shallow snow pockets in the forested areas, and most of the
riverbanks are gripped in ice, the middle of the river rushes past
unchecked on its journey toward Hudson's Bay.

"Word is there's no ice on the St. Lawrence either," Barney
tells me, hoisting one end of a desperately cumbersome thirty-foot

canoe off his car trailer. He gestures to indicate that I should grab
the far end. "If it's a rowing race, we might actually stand a chance
this year."

Barney is one of five members of Calgary's ice canoe team—a
self-described "strong, fit, crazy midget" who rows from the front
end of the boat. Barney has a friendly manner and a contagious
laugh, and soon he's giving me the armchair version of what
racing ice canoes feels like when you're on the river. Imagine
navigating a canoe through a maze of disjointed ice blocks and
powerful currents while bone-chilling winds steal your breath.
At times, temperatures can plummet below minus forty degrees
Celsius, which is the kind of weather that can freeze your fingers
until they're prone to snapping off like icicles. Add to that a pace
that routinely causes participants to reach a heart rate of 180 beats
per minute, sometimes for two hours or more.

"It's pretty much the longest two hours of your life," he explains.
"And if you're not hurtin' you're not workin' hard enough."

Barney and I are soon joined by his colleagues, who help
him carry the 275-pound boat down to the shore. There's Bree,
the beefy, well-spoken captain of the team, possessing a stomach
of iron and shoulders of steel. There's Kale, thin and wiry and
strong; and there's Kevin, who vaguely reminds me of a guitarist
I once saw on a Van Halen video. Finally, there's Jeff with his hip
swagger—either the ladies' man or the class clown; I can't quite
tell at first—who peers out from behind his shades with cowboy
coolness, sniffing at the air.

If the Québécois are sleek, New Age Canotiers de Glace, these guys are the rough and ready ice cowboys.

We find a place not far from shore where the surface ice appears solid, and then clamber out onto the semi-frozen river. The boys stop to adjust their shin pads, strap metal crampons onto their boots for extra traction, and fasten their life jackets.

"Where's a safe place to stand?" I ask Bree, figuring he should be enlightened about these sorts of things after eleven years of racing experience.

"Right where you're standing looks fi..." A sudden explosion of ice and Jeff plunges into thigh-deep water, roughly, oh, ten feet from where I'm standing.

"On the other hand," says Bree, "maybe you'd better stand on shore."

Ten minutes later we're on the river, rowing past Prince's Island, which gives them ample opportunity to fill me in on a bit of history. Ice canoes, it turns out, were first used during the late 1600s for the purpose of delivering mail, food, medicine, and other supplies to island communities in eastern Canada, primarily along Quebec's St. Lawrence River. Boats plied the open water during the summer months, while sleighs were used to cross the river during the winter months. The problem came during freeze-up and break-up, when the mighty St. Lawrence churned with boat-sinking ice blocks.

It's true that the original Canotiers de Glace came from a golden age when men were men, and calling the equipment "rudimentary" would have been generous. "Microsoft" was not a large computer company, but more accurately described the small padded knee braces used to cushion a leg inside the boat while the outer leg scootered with the canoe across rawhide ice. "Megahertz" was what happened if you accidentally dropped the canoe on your foot, or perhaps jammed it between two ice blocks.

Some island communities lay more than ten miles from shore, and many lives were lost while crossing when good weather suddenly turned sour. There's one story of three iceboats travelling to Prince Edward Island in 1885, carrying a load of mail across Northumberland Strait, when a fierce blizzard moved in. All the iceboat captains could do was huddle under their boats and drift aimlessly at sea for three days until they spotted a church steeple through the blowing snow. By this time they had torched all the mail to keep themselves warm; for this hardship, they were awarded six dollars.

These days, of course, mail is no longer at issue. Rather, it's trophies, bragging rights, and a small bundle of prize money at the most legendary of all ice canoe races, the one that takes place at the Carnaval de Québec every year.

Surprisingly, Calgary has the oldest competing team at the race, one that's an anomaly because they're the only out-of-province team (not to mention the only anglophone team). And considering that Calgary has been sending a team to Quebec City every year since 1967, they have maintained one of the most consistent records. In thirty-four years of competition, in fact, they've never won the race. Not once.

The honour has always gone to one of the local teams, and over the last fourteen years, it's been the Anderson brothers and their high-tech Château Frontenac squad that have taken the top prize home twelve times.

"It's pretty hard to win when we're only training on the Bow River," Barney explains as they row. He's referring, of course, to the fact that the St. Lawrence and its unpredictable ice floes and tidal currents are so hard to prepare for.

"And our equipment is usually a few years behind the best stuff they have in Quebec," he adds.

What Barney and his teammates lack in technical skills and equipment, however, they try to make up for with physical conditioning. More often than not, they're among the most physically fit, and they often place in the top two or three teams during the time trials that take place before the competition to queue the teams at the starting gate.

Mind you, winning the race is hardly the main reason for going to Quebec City. There's the challenge of competing at the largest winter festival in the world, and the camaraderie that's shared among ice canoeists—not to mention the pride at being a part of Quebec's riverboat history.

"We get a lot of respect when we go down there," admits Barney. "Mostly because we're honouring men who once risked their lives on the river."

And of course, there are the French girls they meet at Quebec City nightclubs after the race, *les belles filles*, as they're known locally.

"We like the whole carnival atmosphere," says Jeff. "And it wouldn't be a carnival without making an ass of yourself."

*   *   *

With memories of how little patience the French can have for those who don't speak their language, my friend Sheri and I arrive at the Calgary airport three days before the race with plans to learn French during our six-hour flight. Unfortunately, we only manage to get a feel for the basic vocabulary of the winter carnival: *le canot* (the canoe); *saouler et seter* (drinking and partying); *le Bonhomme* (the jolly snowman mascot with a red toque); *Caribou* (not a large deer, but rather a potent mixture of wine and assorted liquors that looks and tastes like antifreeze); and perhaps the most important of all, *la glace* (the ice).

Of course, Quebec's winter carnival comes with ice in many different forms. There's the kind of ice you find along the streets and sidewalks, which makes dodging Quebec taxi drivers remarkably treacherous. (Particularly if they suspect you're an anglophone—anglos are alternatively known as *cahos de vitesse*, or "speed bumps," in Quebec City.) There is the type of ice you can eat, such as *la tire sur neige*, a delectable kind of toffee that results from pouring hot maple syrup onto snow. And for the Canotiers de Glace, there are the many types of ice they have to contend with on the St. Lawrence River: *glace lente* (slow ice); *glace vite* (fast ice); *glace dur* (hard ice); *glace pourie* (rotten ice); and the hated *glace brun* (brown ice), which isn't ice at all, but more like *la tire sur neige* for its ability to stick to a canoe like molasses.

When Sheri and I arrive at the hotel, we're pleased to find that our room comes with a sweeping fourteenth-floor view of old Quebec City and the Plains of Abraham, the very place where the British kicked French keister in 1759, only to let the French keep their city anyway.

Since 1967, it's the Brits who've been getting their keisters kicked out on the St. Lawrence—and with a cold snap forming ice on the river all too rapidly, it's not looking good for that rowing match the Calgary boys had been hoping for.

Ditching our suitcases and hunching into a biting wind, Sheri and I search out dinner. We pass snow sculptures, an ice palace with multicoloured flashing lights, and skaters doing laps on what appears to be a small pond, listening to French folk music. Everywhere—and I do mean everywhere—there are the loud, mournful, agonizing blasts of plastic trumpets bugling into the night air. These emit noises that only a very sick moose could duplicate, but are several times more annoying. We eat dinner at a small French bistro, and then retire happily to our room.

The following day, we meet the Calgary team at the Quebec City marina, which is just downriver from the old town. After taking one look at the swift current and gargantuan ice blocks crunching and heaving and grinding together, Sheri turns to me and says, "They paddle canoes across that? You've got to be kidding!"

"Yeah, I know what you mean," replies Barney. "I remember my first impression of the St. Lawrence. It was kinda like, 'How the hell are we going to get a boat across that?'"

"At least it doesn't give us the heebee-jeebees like it used to," admits Kale.

Kale may be accustomed to these conditions, but my own stomach is none too settled after stepping on board, only to have them drop me on an ice floe in the middle of the river a few minutes later. From this minivan-sized chunk of ice bobbing up the middle of the St. Lawrence is where I plan to get some photos of the team practising (Quebec City's twenty-two-foot tides actually cause the river to flow backwards at times). The vantage point does turn out to be perfect—yet as I snap pictures of the team weaving their way through a matrix of open water, ice blocks, and Slurpee juice, the ice cube I'm standing on begins to tilt precariously sideways.

It's one thing for an ice canoeist go into the drink when the momentum of a moving canoe can yank them back out again; it would be another thing entirely for a journalist to go in when the safety of the boat is a couple of hundred feet away. They rescue me just as I spot a large icebreaker charging up the river toward me at maximum speed.

*   *   *

For some reason, ice canoe racing has traditionally attracted families into its ranks. When the Carnaval de Québec started in 1954, the Lachance brothers were stiff contenders for the first several years. Then came the Gilbert family, with two brothers and a son on one team, while a third brother competed on a second team. Of course, neither of these families compare to the Anderson brothers and their utter domination of the sport. In fact, when their brother Paul wasn't staying in good enough shape, Jean and Jacques kicked him off the team.

When it comes to competing with the big boys in the big race, or even having a shot at winning the big prize, every advantage counts: fitness, training, strategy, equipment. In particular, the technical nature of the sport is a lot more important than one might think.

This becomes abundantly clear to me when I visit Jean and his anglophone teammate Eric Fraser at Château Frontenac headquarters, located inside a large warehouse in a Quebec suburb. When I arrive, they're busy drilling holes to adjust their boat's polyethylene seats and knee braces, and grinding and waxing its polished bottom.

There's no storing this precision craft in a snowbank beside a river barge. "You've got to think of the boat as a giant guitar," Eric explains. "You have to play it a lot before you get a feel for what it can do."

Of course, it also helps to have the proper wax on the bottom of the boat, which depends on the temperature and humidity. Eric tells me that an improperly waxed boat will have 60 to 80 pounds of dynamic drag on fresh snow; a properly waxed boat can get that down to 18 pounds of drag.

As Eric banters, I'm soon lost in explanations of carbo-fluoride wax, triangulation, custom moulds, three-quarter pivot points, and linear equations. Although he's not an engineer like Jean and Jacques, Eric admits that he loves the high-tech aspect of modifying equipment. Jacques has even designed a computer program that analyzes ice conditions on the river, taking into account the tide, current, snow conditions, wind direction, and all other possible parameters.

"It's the only sport I know that involves so much cardio and strength where you can also make an impact on performance through technical data and modifications to your boat," Jacques explains. "It's the complete package sport."

Another reason for the Château Frontenac team's success has been their stringent training regimen. Starting in September, they practice ten to twelve hours every week, and when the ice appears in December, they try to train at the time of day most closely simulating the tidal currents at the time of the race. They spend hours executing turns and pivoting on ice blocks, working in sub-zero temperatures that would make even Canadian postal workers cringe. Add to this the ever-present possibility of ending up in the drink if you misjudge the firmness of a foothold—in fact, while scampering across the ice on his second day, Eric made one of those misjudgements and suddenly found himself up to his neck in slush.

One thing that is clear is just how far the sport has evolved from its early days. The first wooden canoes weighed more than four hundred pounds, far more than the fibreglass and Kevlar boats of today. The clothing of racers has also changed dramatically. Hockey sweaters and hip waders have been replaced by Gore-Tex and neoprene, which keep the participants warmer and marginally more comfortable during their struggle across the ice-choked river.

And what of the sport's culture of competition? "In this sport, we like to share information," Eric tells me. The Château Frontenac team not only spends time practising with other teams, but shares tips on technology and waxing. In particular, they have nothing but good to say about the Calgary boys.

"It means a lot to us that those guys come all the way out here to compete," says Eric. "That's why we like to help them out as much as possible."

*   *   *

Sunday morning dawns with bone-chilling splendour, which is not really a surprise, considering that race day typically dawns with bone-chilling splendour. The St. Lawrence looks downright ominous from the seawall that runs the entire length of old Quebec City. An icy wind is whipping down from the northwest, causing bystanders to huddle against the railing at the marina's mouth as they wait impatiently for the race to start.

The exception to these huddled masses is a gang of two or three hundred enthusiastic cowpokes who have come from western Canada to cheer on the Calgary squad. Every year, as a token of their sister-city friendship, the mayor of Quebec City loans the city's ferry to the fans from Calgary, giving them the perfect place from which to watch the event. When Sheri and I arrive, we find it brimming with festive cheer: white cowboy hats, country music, and line dancing in the cabin deck lounge.

Will this be the year that Calgary finally wins the race?

As is their custom, Calgary has qualified near the front of the pack, and when the pistol is finally fired, all the teams leap out of the starting gate in wild stampede formation. For several moments, it's a scrum to see who can get from the flat marina ice out onto the river. One after another, the dozen or so iceboats round the corner, only to come face to face with a minefield of debris churning upriver on the incoming tidal current.

In the men's elite category, the race consists of two gruelling laps around a five-mile triangular course. The first leg of the race traverses along the seawall to a marker near the ferry platform. This is traditionally the easiest leg, because it often has open water and teams aren't cutting at a precarious angle across the current. From the ferry platform, teams cross to the far side of the river to touch a second buoy, and then race back to the starting gates where the circuit begins all over again.

It should be noted that the buoy on the far side is particularly treacherous to approach, because if a canoe team misjudges the angle and overshoots the marker ever so slightly, it can be impossible to reach it again. Teams that miss the marker sometimes battle against the current for over half an hour just to touch it; if they can't, they're disqualified from the race.

It's not long before the real contenders separate themselves from the stragglers. The Calgary team, hoping for a relatively ice-free river, is greeted instead by slushy pack ice pushed up against the length of the seawall. After they traverse the route along the seawall, crossing the river for the first time proves to be equally challenging. Their progress is painfully slow.

Two or three teams are just reaching Levis for the first time as the Château Frontenac squad blasts along the seawall on their second lap. They reach the buoy, execute a perfect pivot at the ferry landing, and push out into the middle of the current again. Even the second-place team is trailing several hundred yards behind.

The canoes are spread much wider apart on the second lap, and soon the Frontenac squad reaches the far side for a second time, then presses toward the finish line. Nobody is close enough to challenge them. When the times are tallied, they will have finished more than seven minutes before the second-place team.

Of course, this means that the race is already over by the time Calgary and one other team approach the ferry platform on their second lap. Not that it matters. The festive atmosphere is not dulled for one moment. Some cowpokes continue line dancing, while others crowd the ferry deck to chant: "Calgary! Calgary! Calgary!"

As the team approaches the finish, they drag their canoe onto a huge ice block, where they stop, then turn and wave to the adoring fans. The crowd roars with approval.

Sheri and I walk down the seawall to the marina to watch the finish, and sure enough, it's the Calgary boys pulling in dead last.

"Why do we do this again?" Kevin pants shortly after sliding across the finish line.

"Hey," says Jeff, smacking his knuckles against Barney's palm, "it doesn't matter whether we win or lose—we still booze!"

As the racers exchange hugs and high-fives with some of the French teams, beer cans begin flying through the air into outstretched hands. Bree lifts Kale's shirt to inspect a broken rib, courtesy of a fall against one of the canoe's gunwales.

The snow starts to fall in huge popcorn flakes later that evening, and all the ice canoe teams rendezvous for the awards ceremony and to swap stories from the river. The fact that the Anderson brothers and their team are again walking home with top honours is no surprise, but that doesn't dim anybody's enthusiasm. Particularly undimmed is a glowing Jacques Anderson—one would think the novelty of winning would wear off after fifteen years, but it obviously hasn't, if the dips and moves he and Jean pull on the dance floor are any indication.

Meanwhile, Kale nurses his broken rib, and once he's good and liquored up, we all head out to the Quebec nightclubs, which prove to be the best reason for an Albertan to join Calgary's ice canoe team. It's payoff for all those months of sweat, toil, and icy resolve.

This ultimately leads to antics that can't be fully disclosed, lest I break a cardinal rule: Whatever happens in Quebec City stays in Quebec City. I will only say that it involves one unidentified member of the Calgary team *en train de danser sur une table en portent rien qu'un soutien gorge rose* (which, loosely translated, means "dancing bare-chested on a table while wearing a pink bra").

Mind you, it is Quebec City, and it is the Carnaval de Québec, which just happens to be the perfect place for an ice cowboy to celebrate French history while making an ass of himself.

Matt Jackson is president of Summit Studios. He has written more than one hundred magazine articles and is the author of the award-winning book, The Canada Chronicles: A Four-Year Hitchhiking Odyssey. *He claims that standing on an ice floe in the middle of the St. Lawrence to get pictures of Calgary's ice canoe team is one of the crazier things he's done as a journalist.*

A Fish Tale

Our author has a Near Death Experience while sea kayaking in BC's Barkley Sound.

By Terry Gowler

Vancouver Island has to be one of the most wildlife-rich places to explore by sea kayak in North America. The vast array of eagles, whales, sea lions, and other marine wildlife is simply staggering.

Four friends and I had spent a week paddling the Barkley Sound area, and had just finished the last leg of our trip, crossing from Gilbert Island to the docks at Sechart. While it was sad to be leaving such a beautiful place, we were looking forward to a hot meal, showers, and getting cleaned up for the trip home.

Dozens of other kayakers were on the docks preparing for departure into Barkley Sound. My friend Bob was on my left, kneeling on the dock so he could more easily unload his kayak. On my right was John, squaring away his gear. I stood between them, pulling at my paddling gloves, and gazing back wistfully at the magnificent scenery.

You know, it's a simple thing taking off a glove, done without much thought. Two simple tugs and they generally slide right off. As I slipped off my left paddling glove, however, I felt an unexpected tug on my ring finger. A split second later my gold wedding band launched into the air, arched over the water, and made an insignificant little "ker-plop" as it hit the surface. And sank. Fast.

Shit.

I shouted what was to be the first of many expletives as I watched my ring sink three or four metres to the bottom of the harbour. Bob, who had been a university English professor, looked askance at me as I strung together in one long, continuous sentence a tirade of four-letter words.

If there was an upside to this incident, it was that I could still see the ring after it came to rest. It had landed on the silty bottom a couple of metres from the dock.

I pointed at the water, gasped for breath, and tried to explain in simple words what had just happened. Bob eventually caught sight of the gold band at the bottom of the harbour and put everything together.

Then, in utter disbelief, we watched as a large ocean perch—mistaking my shiny ring for a tasty morsel of food—swam out from the shadows of the dock, scooped up my ring in its mouth and started to swim away.

Bob and I were momentarily stunned. As I started barking out another long string of expletives, some of the other kayakers on the dock turned to stare. They must have wondered who I was and what I was yelling about. "Tourette's Syndrome," some of them probably concluded.

Seconds seemed like minutes as "Jaws" swam in lazy circles, and then started back towards the shady protection of the dock. All

I could do was stand there—dumbstruck and cursing—knowing that a fish had just swallowed my wedding ring. It's hard to imagine a feeling of such utter helplessness until you find yourself in a similar situation.

Just as I assumed this Gollum of a fish was about to disappear, forever, with my precious (sorry about that) ring, to our astonishment it spat it out. Again more four-letter words, but this time happy ones. Once again the ring lay on the harbour bottom, still within sight.

John still had his Polartec paddling suit on, so he offered to dive for my ring. We figured that if I lay down on the dock, held my paddle in the water by one end of the blade and stretched out as far as possible, I could point to my ring with the submerged end. John could then follow my paddle down, locate the ring and snatch it up.

As luck would have it, the tip of the paddle touched bottom just a few dozen centimetres from my ring. Without the aid of mask or fins, John made his first dive; unfortunately he came up empty handed. His attempt did stir up a lot of silt though, so we anxiously waited, praying that when the silt settled my ring would still be visible.

Seconds seemed like hours as slowly, and to my great delight, my shiny gold ring came back into view.

On John's second attempt I could see him grabbing handfuls of the muddy bottom as he groped desperately for my ring. When I thought he must surely be short of air, up he popped, ring held triumphantly in his hand.

I was never so relieved. Any of you who are married—or have a significant other and wear a ring signifying that bond—will understand that this was a Near Death Experience. Can you imagine returning home and saying, "Honey ... uh ... I was out kayaking for a week with the guys and a fish came along and ate my wedding ring. Heh, heh ... honest!"

Compound that unlikely explanation with the fact that I'm married to a spitfire redhead. Thanks, John, for saving my life!

Terry Gowler lives in Mount Vernon, Washington. Ever since his "near death experience," he has been experimenting with various adhesives to prevent this from ever happening again.

Vodka, Dirt Roads, and Caviar

*The makings of the first solo bike ride
across Kamchatka.*

By Marty McLennan

I was still lost when I found the white-haired, white-bearded Genady. My pocket map told me I was in the main market of Petropavlovsk Kamchatskiy in Russia's easternmost province and some ten thousand kilometres from home. My mountain bike's odometer showed three thousand and twenty-eight kilometres, and my journal entry was dated June 12. Yet when I thought about who I was and where I was headed, I realized I was just as lost as the day I'd begun this odyssey two-and-a-half years earlier at a bar on the corner of St. Laurent and Bagg streets in Montreal.

It was graduation night, and my girlfriend and I wanted more from post-university life than the inevitable unemployment or nine-to-five jail cell. We thumbed through an atlas in search of escape—a ski adventure was our alibi, but distance from home and self-discovery were the lures. By evening's end, we had decided on the snowy Japanese Alps, and we drank to Nagano as our starting point. We set out on Christmas Day. Over those winter months in the highest part of the Land of the Rising Sun, we worked, skied, fell in love, and then later broke apart. By springtime, she had returned to Montreal.

I wasn't ready for home. Restless and with nothing more to lose, I packed my bags and went in the opposite direction—to the heart of China's Gobi Desert. There I spent half a year hitchhiking on the Silk Road and doubling back across China to the Pacific coast. By the time I reached Shanghai, I had developed a new plan: to return to Canada by bike. I would follow the path of the ancient Chinese and Japanese who trailed caribou from Asia to North America across the Bering land bridge to become North America's First Nations. I would do it on two wheels (with a little help from Aeroflot) because, unlike the ancient Asians, I didn't have centuries to make this migration. I gave myself six months.

I bought a $150 mountain bike in Shanghai and ferried it back across to Japan. I spent another winter in the Japanese Alps skiing and studying topographic maps of the Russian Far East and, in particular, Kamchatka. Instinctively, I knew that of the four countries I would cycle through—Japan, Russia, the United States, and Canada—Russia would demand the most physical and emotional energy. Russian bureaucracy, in fact, was my first hurdle—officials hesitated to grant my visa. Kamchatka was home to two top-secret Russian military installations, including the long-range-missile base rumoured to be the inspiration for Ian Fleming's *You Only Live Twice*. Aside from fearing me as a possible spy, albeit a young one (I was twenty-five years old) the Russians worried for my personal safety. There were plenty of good reasons: no one had ever done this before, I spoke no Russian, the Mafia were making headlines in the area, brown bears roamed the river valleys, and spewing volcanoes spattered the landscape with ash. To survive, I had to be able to live off the land, but I was a lousy fisherman and had no hunting skills. Worst of all, the road was unpaved.

On the plus side, Kamchatka's world-famous salmon runs appealed to my appetite, seismic activity meant soothing hot springs, and the mountainscapes would be incredible. After a two-month wait, my visa application was accepted, and I was able to set my sights on being the first to solo-cycle across the Kamchatka Peninsula.

*   *   *

Spring had come late, and the Russian road oozed mud. To make matters worse, mosquitoes and black flies swarmed me. I had cycled for a week and was trapped by floodwaters on the Pacific coast. A couple of teenagers offered to help me cross a mountain-fed stream. Midway across, they dropped the bike and swung a machete to free my belongings. Adrenaline took over as, bare-fisted and alone, I chased them across the stream and plains. When I finally caught my breath, I felt imprisoned and scared, and I was still fifteen hundred kilometres away from North America. By the time I reached the marketplace, shell shock had taken over.

Genady saw that I was on my last legs. He was a sight himself, with white hair and beard sparkling in the afternoon sun and a three-kilogram salmon hung loosely from his shoulder. His robin's-egg-blue eyes flashed genius, and his soulful laugh shook the plywood walls of the kiosk. As I strained to bargain for a fish, Genady stepped in and negotiated a reasonable price. He asked where I was sleeping, and when I gestured to my tent, he shook his head emphatically, insisting that I stay with his family.

Tucking two bottles of vodka under his arm, Genady led me to his apartment. *"Moy dom vash dom,"* he repeated. *My home is your home.* Flashing a smile, he motioned for me to sit on a kitchen stool while he filleted the salmon and dropped it into a frying pan. He turned back to me, eyes shining, and opened the first bottle. He poured the clear liquid into chipped cups and raised his into the air, waiting for me to follow suit. Smiling broadly, he crossed himself and downed the contents in one gulp. *"Das Bogam,"* he intoned. *God be with us.*

The art of drinking and surviving Russian vodka was the first of many skills I would have to master. Although Genady taught me how to fish for the spawning salmon, how to prepare red caviar, and what military areas to avoid, this one was by far the most important. We sat down at seven that evening, and by two in the morning, we had finished both bottles. Armed with a phrase book, pencil, paper, guitar, and vodka, Genady and I talked and sang the entire night away. In the confines of a strange home in one of the world's most remote areas, I felt surprisingly secure.

*   *   *

The next day, we left the city to spend a week at his family's *dacha* (cottage). Here I learned the true hardships of Russian peasantry. Since the fall of the Communist regime, the average worker no longer had a pension and rarely a paycheque. Genady, a government art teacher, had not been paid in five months. He chuckled at the situation, speaking in charades and making crazy facial expressions, but his financial situation was no laughing matter. For survival, he had to collect berries and mushrooms, grow potatoes and vegetables, and fish. Together with his wife and son, we worked his fields, rebuilt the roof of his house, fished the rivers, and repaired my bike, tent, and courage. Every evening, we wound down with an ice-cold bottle of vodka, fresh bread, and caviar, and we played his guitar and sang.

Before I left on an overcast June day, the four of us sat down in silence—a Russian departure custom called *preciest na darozhku*. After a short time, Genady stood up and passed me a fishing rod and one dozen boiled eggs. *"Shastlivogo puti,"* he said. *Be safe.* When I politely refused, he insisted in his best broken English, "Take zis, zee road eez lonke."

The road was long and sometimes lonely, but each day was punctuated by warm-hearted Russians who skidded their Ladas to a halt. A hearty salutation and handshake were always followed by a language and cultural lesson that went something like this:

"Dobry dien." *Good day.*

I would respond likewise.

"Kuda ty #%@& idiosh?" *Where (expletive) are you going?*

I would answer, *"Ust Kamchatsk."*

They would shake their heads and stare in disbelief.

"Plokhaya doroga!" *The road is bad!*

Then their eyes would inevitably open: *"Chut chut?"* (the invitation for a glass of moonshine).

"Das Bogam!"

*   *   *

The darkened sky hid the morning sun as the Siberian winds rattled the cracked windowpanes and whistled through the planks. Out on the edge of a thirty-two-kilometre spit of land between river and raging Okhotsk Sea, a dozen Russian fishermen and I waited. The black clouds rolled in, and we poured another round of vodka. In the confines of this dingy house, I learned another lesson in Russian life: patience.

They had found me shivering on the doorstep four days earlier. It was two weeks since I had left Genady's *dacha* and I was soaking wet, with my tattered mountain bike and drenched panniers, seeking shelter from the rains. I desperately needed to get warm.

The Russians awaited the coming of the *chavycha*, the king salmon. But the storm had delayed the spawning run, so the men's nets were empty. I also had to wait for better weather, since I was beginning the final stretch of navigable road on my way to Ust Kamchatsk. Only I wasn't as patient as the fishers or their prey.

In the eight-room hut equipped with kitchen, mess hall, billiards room, and cots for twenty men, we waited together, smoking Bulgarian tobacco, swatting mosquitoes, and drinking. The men discussed politics over vodka with rye-bread chasers.

Another one-dollar bottle was emptied, another fisherman snored deeply. Stained teacups, an unfinished chess game, and a half-eaten loaf of bread remained on the dining table.

Needing a break, I walked to the outhouse, lifting my collar against the pelting rains. The old boards croaked in protest at the gale-force winds outside. Fragments of poetry were scattered on the muddied floor—the pages of Tolstoy used for the least glorious execution. Pinned up with a rusty nail, Anton Chekhov's words also fought the winds.

The path back to the sailors' shack was strewn with billowing grasses. A single salmon washed onto the shore, dead before spawning. I watched as crows ate its eyeballs. The dogs curled up against the outer walls of the house and whimpered, waiting for scraps of bread and fish from the kitchen. In my mind, I could see my new Russian friends trudging back to the mess hall. There they would open the door, light up cigarettes, and eat bread without butter, waiting for the fish to come. When the evening's last bottle was drunk, father and son would lie together on a metal mattress. They dreamed of better days ahead.

But I didn't have time to dream. I set off, blue-lipped and shivering. My wheels churned the syrupy road, and I struggled for days against bitter arctic rains. A rickety old sedan, its windshield wipers flapping wildly, pulled up from behind. "Get in!" the men frantically motioned—it was three of the fishermen. The driver switched the heat to full blast and gave me dry clothes to change into. He stepped out into the rain and lifted the engine hood.

Meanwhile, the men crammed into the back seat offered me a shot of vodka. Closing the door, the driver proudly announced a special roadside surprise. He unwrapped the metre-long tinfoil package—a fried fillet of king salmon kept warm by engine heat, the first catch of the season. As we feasted together on the succulent meat, the driver gestured for me to return to the brigade house. But by now, my dream was in sight—I was halfway through Kamchatka, and as crazy as it seemed to them, I had only a thousand kilometres to the end of the road.

Michael, the youngest of the fishers, gave me a wool hat his mother, the cook, had knit for me. *"Vozmi, tebe budet kholodno,"* he called from the moving car, shouting and waving encouragement on the desolate road. *Take, you are cold.* As they disappeared into the grey horizon, I repeated what Genady had taught me—being at home is a state of mind. I was considerably warmer when I replaced my helmet with the woollen hat.

*   *   *

The skies cleared for the final month of my trip, and I was rewarded as the tundra gave way to lush alpine vegetation. Biking was still no picnic, but natural hot springs, fresh campfire salmon steaks, and occasional bear sightings complemented my riverside nights.

At the northernmost part of the road, I came face to face with my pre-trip nemesis: the top-secret long-range-missile base in

Klyuchi. The guards, starved by boredom and bitten with curiosity, laughed at my papers. They wondered who in his right mind would want to come out here. When they found out I was Canadian, they greeted me with bear hugs and a shot of vodka, which was drunk to my questionable mental health. Even in the remotest part of Russia, they had seen enough James Bond films to realize that spies don't travel on mountain bikes, looking like drowned rats. Nevertheless, I was able to acquire top-secret information: the base has an indoor tennis court, and the guards are better hosts than doubles partners.

Backdrop to the missile site was the perfectly symmetrical Klyuchevskaya volcano. At 4,750 metres, it is the largest volcano in Eurasia and one of the most active, last spewing lava and smoke in 1993. By good fortune, I was able to explore a parasitic cone with several volcanologists. Halfway up the enormous mountain at sunset, I lay in a hammock and was hit by a waft of elation. Before falling asleep, I scribbled six short words in my journal: August 28. Klyuchevskaya. I made it!

Although Klyuchevskaya is beautiful to the eyes, its recent eruption wreaked havoc on the roads—the last two hundred kilometres, from Klyuchi to Ust Kamchatsk, were washed out by volcanic sand. No longer able to ride, I pushed my two-wheeled Winnebago over the seismic ash and through swarms of black flies. After three years on the road and innumerable meetings with people—from knife-wielding crooks to world-famous geologists— I had a good idea of who I was and what I was made of. When I studied the road and my condition and thought about my dream of being the first to cycle the Kamchatka Peninsula, I knew it was fated that I not complete this leg of the trip.

Depending one last time on Russian hospitality, I flagged down a passing truck. Broad-smiling Sacha swaggered out of his beaten yellow rig. "Impossible...," he said in a thick Russian accent, inspecting my heavily loaded bike and mosquito-eaten flesh. "Russian road, impossible...."

As I bounced along the washboard gravel road in the Ukrainian-built truck, my jangled mind recalled the months of solo-cycling through Russia's easternmost frontier. I sat mesmerized by the finality of my Russian journey. Sacha interrupted my thoughts. *"Fchira ...,"* he began, singing the first verse of the Beatles' *Yesterday* in Russian. I joined in as we passed Klyuchevskaya, on our way home. Without missing a beat, he pointed out the silhouette of a low-flying owl and winked, as if to say, "Russian road, incredible... Russian road, incredible."

Over the weeks and months to come, my bike and I would venture through some incredible places—across Alaska, through the Gulf Islands, and across British Columbia. Every morning before setting out, I would sit in silence, as I did with Genady's family. My thoughts went out to my Russian friends. Biking through Kamchatka taught me the most important lesson: In the end, it doesn't matter where you are, who you are with, or what you are doing. The only thing that really matters is who you are.

Over the past decade, Marty McLennan has managed to ride his bike halfway around the planet. When not biking he has worked as photo editor at Equinox, Harrowsmith, Canadian Wildlife *and* Wild *magazines. He has also freelanced his writing and photography to some thirty magazines, ranging from Argentina to England. At present he is taking some time out of the saddle to work on a PhD in the philosophy of technology.*

Tying the Knot

Wedded bliss in Canada's Rocky Mountains.

By Rick Kunelius

I took it all in stride when a client of mine, Keith Hannah, stopped the wedding march and announced that the ceremony for him and his bride-to-be would take place "right here." It seemed of little consequence that *here* happened to be one pitch from the summit of 11,000-foot Mount Hector, at the edge of a precipice plummeting several thousand feet into Banff's Bow Valley.

We had started the wedding procession in the wee hours of the morning, after sleeping in tents at the toe of a large glacier the previous night.

So why did the groom want to stop "here and now?" Because it was exactly eight o'clock in the morning, and at exactly eight o'clock the previous year he had proposed. At exactly eight o'clock the year before that, he had first expressed love for his bride. Nothing else mattered.

As a Banff-based marriage commissioner and former National Park warden, I marry more than one hundred couples every year. This ceremony was hardly the most arduous or unusual one that I've taken part in. In fact, a number of candidates could vie for that title. While aiding in the exchange of wedding vows, I am as likely to find myself hiking, skiing, or whitewater rafting as I am to find myself hanging off the side of a mountain. There's never a dull moment, I can assure you.

I once used a mule as an unofficial wedding witness, and on another occasion I had to stop the ceremony when a herd of bighorn sheep marched obliviously through the proceedings. Another time I turned around to see a determined ground squirrel munching happily on the bridal bouquet. Fortunately, I've never had a grizzly bear object to anyone getting married. They can be fairly persuasive.

One of the most memorable weddings was the day I held a service on the glacier-capped summit of Mount Temple, the tenth-highest peak in the Canadian Rockies. When I came to the part where the bride is supposed to say "I do," she took one look at her man, one look at the five thousand feet of air beneath us, and said "Freakin eh!"

Of course, not all of the weddings I perform are outside. I've also married people in bathing suits. One morning while I was working out at the gym, a couple from Yellowknife found me and asked if I could perform a wedding "on the spot." They were spending the day at the spa, and had their marriage license and a smiling witness. It may have been a little noisy standing beside the indoor waterfall, but soon they were squeaky clean, refreshed, and married.

It can also be very romantic to get married on skis with large, puffy snowflakes falling all around. Seal the vows with a kiss, and tuck into the strawberries, shrimp cocktail, and champagne. I'll be sure to bring my portable CD player to serenade the happy couple with a little Mozart and Grieg. Once the ceremony has taken place and the food has been eaten, I can honestly assure couples that it's "all downhill from here!"

On the formal wedding documents that go to Edmonton, I take great pleasure in writing the locations of obscure ceremonies. One place at the Lake Louise ski hill has been affectionately dubbed "Altar Alley," because if we're not marrying couples there, we're sacrificing something to the snow gods. The most fun is when I have to use the name of a natural landmark or the grid coordinates from a topographical map on the wedding documents. I've received more than one suspicious call from government officials who can't believe that some of these places actually exist.

The way I see it, your wedding is the most important contract you'll ever sign, so why make it a sombre occasion? If two people love the outdoors, it just makes sense to have their ceremony outside. My only golden rule is that I deal with the bride and groom only—no mothers-in-law. If the mother-in-law gets involved, I know that it's going to be like signing the Treaty of Versailles.

I've been performing outdoor weddings now for twelve years, and I don't plan to stop marrying people any time soon. I remember one surreal winter ceremony where I skied with the bride and groom across Lake Minnewanka near Banff, Alberta. A full moon was out, bathing the surrounding peaks in a subtle blue light. As the bride and groom began exchanging vows, we could hear wolves howling in the distance.

And that, my friends, is why I got into this business!

Rick Kunelius is a Banff-based marriage commissioner who loves telling stories almost as much as he loves marrying couples in obscure locations. You can find out more about his business at www.kunelius.com.

Jump

Sometimes a girl has to take a big leap of faith.

By Becky Lynne

The last piece of advice I heard as I stood at the edge of the AJ Hackett Bungy Tower high above the tropical rainforest of Cairns, Australia was, "Keep your eyes straight ahead and jump toward the horizon."

The first piece of advice had been from a fellow traveller who, when I had expressed my ambivalence between excited anticipation and paralyzing fear, told me that when I was up on the platform, the crew would count me down from five. "Just jump before you hear them get to 'one,'" she told me, "or you're likely to lose your nerve."

Five…

Extreme sports were never really my thing. Not to say that I wasn't open to adventure—I had ridden camels around the pyramids of Egypt, climbed Mount Sinai, trekked through the jungles of northern Thailand, and motorcycled across the rocky terrain of Turkey. Indeed, by the age of twenty I had done more travelling than many people do in a lifetime. But to me—a girl from small-town Ontario who was afraid of heights, a girl who had chickened out of riding the kiddie coaster at Canada's Wonderland when I reached the front of the line—bungy jumping felt like a life-threatening and death-defying feat. That kind of dare-devilling and adrenaline-seeking just wasn't in my nature—or so I thought.

Maybe it's Australia's remoteness from the rest of the world that inspires the urge to reach beyond what is known and venture into the mystery and rush of experiencing life to the fullest. Whatever it was, it seemed to be contagious, because after working, living and travelling in the land Down Under, I began to feel the drive to do things that I never would have thought possible. Things like breaking up with the guy whom I assumed I was going to spend the rest of my life with. After fighting all the way through Southeast Asia, it became clear to me that we were bound more by possessive jealousy and passion than we were by love. Still, it was hard to let go, and when we realized that we'd be better off going our separate ways, he left Australia and I was left alone.

Four…

Part of me felt so sad and insecure that I almost bought a ticket for the next plane home. Yet the part of me that had felt stifled by being one half of a couple was excited to be alone and discovering who I was. I decided to embark on a solo adventure from Melbourne up the East Coast to Queensland, and bought a bus pass before fear made me change my mind.

Leaving the flat was easier than I thought. Fuelled by the lack of obligation to the wants, needs and expectations of another, I began to feel liberated and could see the possibilities unravelling before me. I came to discover that one of the many wonders of travelling is that you can never be quite sure how the journey will unfold.

Three…

Another thing I learned about travelling alone in Australia is that you're never really alone—along the way you meet people who have been where you're going or are going where you've been. There is always someone who is sharing the same path as you, even if their journey happens to be taking them in the opposite direction. In the weeks that followed, I submerged myself in the spectacular underwater world of the Great Barrier Reef, sailed around the Whitsunday Islands on an aging eighty-foot schooner called *The Golden Plover*, and spent a lot of time basking in the rays of the glorious Australian sun. The best part of all these experiences was the people I met along the way, people who shared my passion to experience themselves and the world around them, and whose encouragement and inspiration helped me in my quest to make a giant leap of faith.

As my year in Australia was coming to an end, I boarded the bus to Cairns with the intention of hurling myself off a tiny plank from a great height, nothing between me and death but a giant elastic cord tied to my ankles. I must have taken a momentary leave of my senses because the next thing I remember is standing at the top of the bungy tower. It became frighteningly clear that it had all become way too real way too fast, and there were only two ways for me to get down—I could turn around and walk back down the stairs or I could face my fears and jump.

Two…

I jumped. Keeping my eyes straight ahead I leaped, arms outstretched toward the horizon, reaching for an imaginary trapeze so that I could swing against the sky. For a moment I was flying, suspended weightless in mid-air. Nothing else mattered—until gravity kicked in with a force so absolute that there was no negotiating with it. I tried to scream but the air was ripped from my lungs; all that escaped was the "uh" part of "uh oh," and I begin to freefall toward the pond of shallow water below. In what felt like both an eternity and an instant, it became clear that I was headed toward my death and there was nobody who could save me. Then I felt it: tension. The sweet strain of the cord telling me I had fallen as far as I could fall and the only place to go was up.

Then came the giant surge of relief. I was laughing, bouncing, deliriously happy, and hollering like a maniac. I felt more alive than ever.

I was assisted safely to shore, where I sat for some time, mesmerized, as—one after another—travellers climbed to the tower to make their own jumps. I sat until I could sit no longer, then did the only thing you can do once you realize you can push through fear to accomplish a feat you never before thought possible—I climbed back up and did it again.

At the age of eighteen Becky turned down an academic scholarship in favour of spending the next few years travelling and working her way around the world. She eventually returned to Canada and earned a combined degree in drama and psychology. She is currently working on a one-woman show that she hopes will be adapted for television.

Lamb of God

You want me to do what?

By Philip Torrens

It had been a rough voyage, and the ice now blocking my kayak's course seemed like the last straw.

Two of us had left from Toronto nearly three weeks earlier, madly keen to paddle to Montreal. "Madly" seemed the apt word in retrospect: we had set out in mid-March, while the shores of Lake Ontario were still white with snow. We'd been stormbound for days at a time, been forced to attempt siege-like landings on ice-covered shores, and had even had a tent destroyed in a sleety storm.

A week into the trip, my companion, plagued by back and hand ailments, had been forced to call it quits. Since then, I'd pressed on alone. To be sure, I'd enjoyed some good moments—exhilarating launches where I simply tobogganed in my loaded kayak down frozen embankments into the water, and a trance-like hour kayaking through water so calm that the approaching headland seemed suspended in space and time.

I'd also had bad moments. There was a near fatal "shortcut" across the mouth of a wide bay that had taken me out of the land's lee, from where I had barely managed to claw back to shore through the teeth of the wind. There were evenings when I landed so sheathed in ice that I had to hammer both my life jacket and my boat's hatch covers with my paddle before they could be removed.

That morning, I'd broken camp and set out, cheered by the calm, sunny weather, and by the prospect of landing in Kingston in the next day or two. I'd decided to cut the trip short at Kingston for one primary reason. If paddling a large, icy lake was foolish, paddling the St. Lawrence—a large ice-choked river—would have been lunacy.

By mid-afternoon, I'd reached the channel between the mainland and Amherst Island, which sprawled long and low on my right. To my surprise and dismay, the channel was blocked by ice. I'd encountered lots of large ice chunks on previous days, but they'd been loosely scattered and easy to work through. Here, they were tightly packed, stacked together by the prevailing wind, or perhaps by the outflow to the nearby St. Lawrence. I followed the only lead, which zig-zagged through the pack like a lightning bolt before coming to a dead end two kilometres later. With the short afternoon wearing on, I was increasingly nervous about the ice suddenly shifting and trapping me. Discouraged, I backtracked to the island.

Once beached, I noticed a small farmhouse through the trees. I trudged up to the house to ask for water and to inquire about camping on their land. I was greeted with true charity by the husband, Ian, and was offered not only water, but supper and a bed for the night. After a good home-cooked meal, I drifted off to sleep beneath a comforter in a brass-framed bed. I was warm and my stomach was full, so it didn't take long.

The next day the ice looked as treacherous as it had the day before, but my hosts seemed happy to let me stay. Determined to earn at least part of my keep, I followed Ian out to the barn to see how I might be of use. Our first task was to break bales of straw to scatter on the floor—it was lambing season and the ewes needed fresh bedding.

As a city kid, I hadn't seen a live birth before, so I watched in fascination. In contrast to the Sturm-und-Drang that television had conditioned me to expect, what was striking about the ewes was their complete equanimity towards, indeed, indifference to, the miracle of birth. They would stand, placidly munching on food, while baby dropped out the stern. Sometimes, the lamb would begin to emerge misaligned, so Ian would have to shove it back from whence it came and rearrange it a bit to avoid damage to mother and child.

Once, as he was thus engaged, a second "misbirth" started a metre away. Ian waved me over, and thrust me into the breach, as it were. Nervous as I was—an intern performing his first examination—I was shortly elbow-deep in my endeavour. I glanced anxiously towards the mother-to-be's face to see if I was hurting her. She was not missing a beat, or, rather, a bite. (However, based on this experience, whenever I've jocularly suggested to human females that they're making a mountain out of a molehill regarding the birth process, the notion has been coldly received at best.)

A few moments after I withdrew my arm, the lamb emerged

safely into the world. I watched with a pleased and proprietary air as she struggled to stand, wobbling like a bagpipe on puppet strings.

It was then that the epiphany struck.

"The Lord is my Shepherd..." Even to people like me, not raised in a Christian household, these words are familiar. So familiar, we rarely give them much thought. They invoke a pleasantly pastoral image, often depicted in prayer-book pictures or stained-glass windows. But now, with the force of revelation in my arms, my understanding of these words leapt from abstract to literal. It was an emotional experience.

As I cradled the helpless lamb, I understood how powerful the shepherd metaphor would have been to the actual shepherds of Biblical times. They would have believed that God was to them as they were to their flocks: infinitely wiser and more powerful, and, as a result, capable of infinite compassion. They would have understood the introduction to the 23rd Psalm in a way unattainable to modern urban dwellers, Christian or not. I sat there, rocking the lamb, suffused in a warm glow, richer in my head and in my heart for the experience.

It is in search of moments like these that I travel. By definition, you cannot know what you do not know, so you cannot seek such moments directly. You can only set the stage and prepare your mind by sweeping aside, however temporarily, ordinary concerns. I find the best way to do this is to travel, preferably under my own power. A single instant of such insight is worth weeks of what some might consider deprivation and hardship.

Now if this were a fictional tale, after birthing the lamb I would have immediately, and permanently, become a true believer. But it's a real-life story. I was, and still am, an agnostic—not prepared to embrace a belief merely because it is vastly appealing. Intellectual honesty requires proof, not mere faith. That same intellectual honesty also requires me to acknowledge the impossibility of proving that God is not real, which is why I am agnostic rather than atheist.

Still, while I may not believe in a divine being, I now understand the belief better, and why people believe it. Perhaps, not to sound arrogant, I even understand one aspect of that belief better than some believers themselves. And that's a lot to have learned from a lamb.

Though the events of this story happened many years ago, Phillip's passion for paddling continues unabated. He works for a major outdoor retailer while penning freelance articles about his many adventures on the side. He thinks of this trip fondly every time he eats roast lamb.

Of Yaks and Men

Get out of the way, because yaks wait for no man!

By Conor Grennan

There are two basic rules one should observe while hiking through the Himalayas: don't ascend too quickly, and make sure yaks pass you on the cliff side of the narrow trails. They're called "rules" because you are bound to live longer if you abide by them. You need to walk slowly in order to acclimatize, just as you should always press yourself against the mountain when you see over-laden yaks bearing down on you, their horn-studded heads swaying side to side, threatening to gore you in the ass.

This second rule became all too clear on day two of a multi-day trek up to the Mount Everest Base Camp. I was with my German friend Chris, plus Nancy and Jay, a Canadian couple we'd met the previous day. It was some time around mid-morning when we arrived at our first suspension bridge, which was swinging precariously over the raging Dudh Kosi River. Four pairs of white-knuckled hands clutched the side cables of the bridge as we began to inch across it. It lurched sickeningly to the left, and then swung recklessly down and back up to the right.

Thankfully, it only took a few minutes to get accustomed to the sway and conquer our vertigo—so much so, in fact, that we even started swinging it ourselves, snapping dramatic photos as we meandered across the narrow span. I was in front, and about halfway across I decided to stop and take a photo of our porter, Purba, who had already reached the other side. Purba, apparently eager to ham it up for the camera, immediately got into the act; he started jumping up and down and waving excitedly from the far side. I took his picture and waved back. Then another porter, on the same side as Purba, started jumping up and down and yelling at us from a hundred metres away. I assumed he wanted his picture taken, too, and I was more than happy to oblige.

"Man, these guys love having their pictures taken!" Nancy called out from behind me.

"Don't I know it!" I yelled back.

It was around that time, dear readers, that a disturbing realization dawned on me. Those friendly porters were not, in fact, leaping up and down to show off for the camera. They could not have cared less about having their mugs on film. No, they were waving that frantic wave for an entirely different reason. Behind the second porter, I suddenly spotted a long procession of yaks rambling down the slope. Toward the narrow, swaying bridge. The one we were standing on. With big backpacks.

Correctly translated, Purba's frantic waving was, in fact, trying to tell us: "Get the hell off the bridge, 'cause yaks wait for no man!"

As a result, the majesty of our first spectacular river crossing ended rather abruptly with the four of us breaking into a full sprint toward the far side of the desperately swinging bridge as the yaks closed in on it. I got across first, a few metres before the first of the yaks. Heroically, I jumped in front of the lead yak, waved my arms wildly and yelled "Bwaaaa!" in its big old yak face in a pathetic attempt to slow it down. Then I jumped out of the way. Chris got across a second later and yelled a slightly more Germanic version of "Bwaaaa!" before throwing himself out of the way, too.

Nancy and Jay weren't so lucky. A couple of seconds later they found themselves staring at the horns of six determined yaks snorting and scuffling across the bridge. Somehow, they managed to press themselves against the side cable and stay on the bridge—I'm not quite sure how—as thousands of pounds of yak payload barrelled past them. And somehow, quite miraculously, they were spared.

We all collapsed on the far side of the bridge for a few minutes of silence, all of us breathing heavily. When I finally looked up, I saw Purba staring at me with a puzzled expression on his face.

"What you say to yaks?" he asked.

"Oh … well … nothing, really. I guess I said 'Bwaaaa!'"

He said nothing for a minute, and then exploded with laughter. It was tough to tell if he thought the whole thing was genuinely hilarious, or whether he was just ecstatic that his employer hadn't been gored and rutted off a suspension bridge on day two of the trek. Either way, we had learned two things that morning: this trek was going to be much tougher than anticipated, and Purba had a sense of humour.

*   *   *

The Nepali wilderness is overwhelmingly gorgeous in every direction—if you gave a point-and-click camera to a chimp he'd still come back with *National Geographic*-calibre photos. But much more than that, the country has a way of making you feel small but not insignificant, tiny but blessed; you follow the trail feeling like a spectator in a parade of giants. Prayer flags and Buddhist Mani stones (large boulders tattooed with dark Nepalese writing) decorate the sacred pathway. Trekkers and climbers have been using these trails for decades, and the steady stream of visitors from far away places has become a permanent part of Sherpa life.

Our third day in the mountains was a mandatory altitude acclimatization day for trekkers, so we stayed in the market town of Namche Bazaar. At altitudes above three thousand metres or so, one needs to remain at the same altitude for a day or two, especially after a rapid ascent. This gives the body an opportunity to create new red blood cells to cope with the lower density of air molecules, which accounts for a diminished overall level of oxygen getting into your lungs.

At least, that's what I'd read. In reality, this rather technical definition conveys almost nothing about what being at altitude actually feels like. The feeling of breathlessness is completely and utterly stifling. To illustrate the point, imagine falling asleep in your bed, breathing a little too deeply, and accidentally sucking an entire quilt into your lungs. Got it? Right. Now imagine yourself panicking because you just sucked down a goddamn quilt, and as you're desperately gasping for air, you accidentally suck down *another* quilt, plus a bunch of couch cushions and your girlfriend's cat. Then jump on a Stairmaster for about eight hours, and you've pretty much got the gist of what being at altitude *feels* like.

If that isn't bad enough, being at altitude also seems to have a downright unfair effect on one's bladder, shrinking it down to about the size of a hazelnut. If you don't like getting up in the middle of the night to pee, then being at altitude is not for you, my friend. Imagine this scenario: having to get up in the pitch black at thirty-three hundred metres, in the middle of winter, and then having to navigate down some perilous steps and across a yak enclosure to find an invisible outhouse. Not fun.

For some reason I had convinced myself I was going to stay in my sleeping bag that night no matter what my bladder was telling me. As it turned out, however, my bladder is prone to mutiny in situations like this, and clenching one's eyes shut doesn't mean that one is going to fall back to sleep. I tried to remain perfectly still for as long as possible, but I was fighting a losing battle; eventually I kicked off my sleeping bag and stomped out the door, which led directly outside into the night. It was a black and moonless night, so I peered around in the darkness, not even sure where the damn outhouse was located.

This was too much. I was freezing and there was nobody around, and by God, if there is one fundamental male right, it is the right to pee wherever you're standing. With no small sense of self-righteousness, I leaned out as far as I could from the stone platform on which my little room stood and let fly. My shivering shoulders sagged with the expected relief.

What was less expected was the sudden and explosive snorting that shattered the silence just below the wall, followed immediately by a kind of loud and mournful *mooing* sound. It was only then I realized I was peeing directly onto a yak, completely invisible in the dark. I swear I jumped a country mile—I practically sucked the stream of pee right back into my urinary tract. It scared the holy bejeezus out of me, as it probably did the yak. Though in fairness, I was lucky to be simply scared … not scared and getting pissed on.

Back in my sleeping bag a few minutes later, I recalled the yak-induced terror of the bridge just a couple of days before. I smiled. I couldn't help feeling I'd scored a point for our team.

*   *   *

At high altitude, the weather can change quickly and often quite predictably—mornings are crystal clear, the clouds roll in during the afternoon, and the nighttime clears again to reveal an unobstructed view of the heavens.

We trudged into the tiny Sherpa village of Tengbouche, located at just under four thousand metres and situated on a small plateau. From a hundred metres away we could just make out a grand monastery resting heavily in the mist, dominating the immediate landscape. Come the next morning, though, the fog had lifted and the monastery was dwarfed by the staggering size of Mount Everest, covering half the brilliant blue sky and putting everything else into perspective, including how far we still had to walk.

Any notion that we were slowly adjusting to the altitude vanished with the trees at around four thousand metres. The landscape, which only hours earlier had been a lush rhododendron forest, was now a barren moonscape. The altitude and the headwind coming down the valley kept us moving at a pace that, if we had been forced to race all God's creatures in the Judgment Day Olympics, would have placed us in the slowest heat, competing against dead badgers and sea sponges.

After a two-day acclimatization in the little village of Pheriche, we set off at our same sloth-like pace, eventually reaching Lobuche, the highest camp we would occupy, perched at just under five thousand metres. It was from here that we would make our final climb.

We had decided that instead of trekking to Everest Base Camp itself, which is apparently a rather dull place (and what a great time to tell us that), we would climb an additional five hundred metres above Base Camp to the summit of Kala Pattar. It was here, we were told, that we would be afforded the best views.

And so it was that at about 5:45 A.M., seven days after starting the trek, Chris and I crawled out of our sleeping bags and faced our gazillionth bowl of porridge. We knocked enough ice from the freezing stream to wash ourselves, and set out the door with Purba on the coldest morning yet, heading up the valley toward looming Mount Everest.

The sun didn't hit us until about an hour later, as the first spears of light illuminated a mountain of boulders, dumped there millions of years before by the glacier. These rocky moraines would become the terrain for the rest of our journey. It was a completely different landscape, one that left trekkers and yaks alike scrambling for footholds in the loose shale, all the way to the last, lonely outpost before Base Camp, known as Gorak Shep. We paused there only for a brief rest before tackling the final and most challenging part of the entire trek—climbing Kala Pattar.

It was a long, steep trek up that final dark-rock slope: literally breathtaking. But the view from the top was worth it. It was, quite simply, the best view I have ever experienced in my life. I forgot how tired I was, how little air there was to breathe, and how the high-altitude sun was scorching all parts of my face not shielded by my wrap-around sunglasses (thus ensuring I would look like a photo negative of Zorro for the next two weeks).

On one side, the glacial lakes gathered together in pools of impossible turquoise, the ice tumbling off the mountains like child's blocks off the kitchen table. From the direction we had come, we could see the Khumbu Glacier snaking down the valley, carrying incalculable tons of rock and ice, ripping apart the valley in slow motion. The Khumbu Icefall, one of the most treacherous segments of Everest's most popular climbing route, spilled down the mountain like a bag of crushed ice that had toppled over and split open, left for somebody else to clean up. And to the east was Mount Everest itself, with Base Camp at its feet—the camp visibly marked by the black wreckage of a Russian cargo plane that had crashed two years prior.

Yet it was the pinnacle of Everest, a wide dark pyramid marking the highest point on Earth, which held our gaze and sank beneath our skin.

As the three of us sat together on the peak of Kala Pattar, surrounded by a tangled web of new and tattered prayer flags, I felt like I used to feel when my father carried me on his shoulders. It was a different world from above, intoxicating in every way. I remembered hearing about an astronaut who almost died on a space walk—he was reluctant to come back into the space shuttle because the view of Earth was so perfect. That's how I felt, like I could have stayed up there until the clouds filled the valley and the mountain froze. You don't leave a place like that so much as you tear yourself away.

*   *   *

All it took was two mouthfuls of grease-smeared fried potatoes that night in Lobuche to realize I had made a terrible mistake.

Those bacteria-poisoned potatoes, I knew, were going to ravage my insides, and they weren't going to wait long to do it. It seemed terribly unfair after what we had gone through that day. Not to mention that I was just coming down off an altitude-induced headache, which happen to be notoriously painful. These headaches are similar to normal headaches, but have a few upgraded features that make them feel like somebody has stuffed your cheeks with live grenades and yanked out the pins.

But the headache was just that: a headache. It would go away. It was the combination of altitude sickness and the devastatingly unsanitary cuisine that was about to make my life absolutely miserable.

We went to bed early that night, exhausted from the day's climb. I woke up about an hour after dozing off and knew immediately I was going to be sick. For some people, that's not the end of the world—you get up, get sick, go back to bed. For me, though … well, let's just say I don't do "getting sick" with a whole lot of dignity. I tend to lie in bed until the last possible second, then lunge for the bathroom, throwing myself at the mercy of the toilet bowl. So you can perhaps imagine my consternation when, after extracting myself from my sleeping bag, I had to throw on every piece of clothing and sprint outside to hurl on the mountain in sub-zero temperatures.

As a humiliating bonus, I realized the exterior walls of our shelters were wafer-thin. Essentially, it was like getting up in front of a blissfully drowsy audience, taking out a megaphone, and screaming that unique *Blaaaaah!* sound that draws universal sympathy from anybody within earshot. There's no chance people are going to mistake it for anything but some dude blowing chunks. It was more than a little embarrassing, and I realized with even more consternation that it wasn't going to be over quickly.

So I lay there under the stars for hours, as miserable as I've ever been, knowing in my gut that one of the worst days of my life was looming ahead. Altitude sickness can be fatal if one does not descend immediately, and I knew that at first light Chris and I would have to wake Purba and descend to the Himalayan Rescue Association in the small village of Pheriche. This would have been a difficult enough challenge when I was healthy, let alone when I couldn't even ingest water.

What could I do but accept my fate?

Still, I had accomplished what I'd set out to do that day. I had climbed Kala Pattar, I had seen Everest's majesty, and the deep satisfaction I felt from that was so great that the price I was paying—shivering and spewing my guts on that hill—seemed insignificant. The stars at that altitude were clearer than I'd ever seen them, as if I'd spent my whole life looking at the night sky through a dirty window.

Then it occurred to me that I would never be here in this place again, maybe never be this high again, this alone, this quiet, this pure, this empty (no pun intended), or this full. Perhaps, I thought, this moment is a watershed moment in my life.

What I did know was I'd have a lot of time to think about it that night. So I rubbed my hands together to warm them up and tried simply to absorb the moment. I listened to the slow heavy footsteps of the yaks grazing nearby, to their bells breaking the silence, and I imagined them levelling their steady, curious gaze at the strange bundled-up white boy who took all of this, and himself, so very seriously.

Conor Grennan is an Irish American who spent eight years working in international public policy in Prague and Brussels before taking eighteen months off to travel. His work can also be found in the travel humor anthologies What Color is Your Jockstrap *and* Tales from Nowhere, *and on his web site: www. conorgrennan.com. Conor has recently volunteered at a rural orphanage in Nepal where he continues to avoid yaks while hiking on high mountain trails.*

Love on the Rocks

How to drown your fiancée in ten easy steps.

By Matt Jackson

My fiancée and I had only been engaged for a week and already our relationship was on the rocks. Specifically, it was on a shoal of sharp, unpleasant rocks in the middle of Ontario's Michipicoten River.

No question about it; we were stuck. Stacey and I had been paddling against the river's brutal current for two days, and at every turn the fast-flowing water had out-muscled us and drained us of resolve. At certain points where it was shallow enough, we had managed to drag the canoe upriver, but here, just beyond the shoal, the river dropped off. Along both shores the swells roiled ominously, and with large trees hanging off the banks, dragging the canoe along the shoreline was no longer an option. We had reached an impasse.

"We have to paddle against the current," I groaned, wiping sweat and dead mosquitoes from my brow.

"What? Are you crazy?" replied my fiancée of five days. One of the things I have always loved about Stacey is her clarity in stressful situations.

"I'm not crazy!" I retorted. "It's our only option. If we try to wade further upriver the current will pick us up and drag us into those rapids."

Not a pretty sight, that. Imagine what life would look like from the inside of a large industrial washing machine, and you'll get a pretty vivid picture of a river scenario gone very wrong.

Stacey just stood there with one of those I-want-to-wrap-my-paddle-around-your-neck smiles that any person adept at non-verbal communication can recognize. But in this case I feared the river more, so her expression did little to convince me that wading upriver was a better option. A paddle around the neck would be merely inconvenient; getting swept away by the river, losing our canoe, and spending three days retrieving gear from several kilometres of muddy shoreline would be torture.

So for the next fifteen minutes we stood in the middle of the current contemplating many things. We stood there contemplating the river, contemplating life, contemplating our engagement—wondering exactly how we were going to get out of this mess. The river roared past us all the while, an unstoppable freight train. It seemed an unbearable thought that we had to spend the next month in a canoe together, paddling seven hundred kilometres from Lake Superior to James Bay.

Then I did some basic math. If we were going to be married for the next fifty years, this was not Day Two of twenty-nine on the river. This was roughly Day Five of eighteen thousand, two hundred and sixty-seven. But then, who was really counting?

*   *   *

I've always been a big fan of metaphors. Not surprisingly then, when I first took up the sport of mountaineering back in the mid-1990s, I quickly gravitated toward the "mountain metaphor" to guide, inform, and offer my life new perspective. As I'm sure you know, the mountain metaphor compares the challenges of ascending a mountain to the art of living one's life. The hardships faced while climbing, for example, correlate to the day-to-day challenges a person faces in his or her career and relationships.

While tackling a challenge (say, a difficult math problem at university) I learned to envision myself hauling ass over a big overhanging ledge. The day-to-day drudgery of accounting classes was henceforth related to ascending five thousand vertical feet of loose, crappy rock. And dating Susie Gilmour was vaguely like being stuck in a frozen tent for three days during a blizzard (we only dated a couple of times). It was a useful metaphor, and it certainly helped get me through the dog days at university.

But then I realized something: who the hell wants to fight gravity all their life? Really, truly, who wants to spend their life trudging up endless rubble slopes, gripping sheer rock faces with white knuckles, and dodging rockfall? And all for five minutes with a decent view at the top? No thanks, *mes amis*, count me out!

Then I discovered paddling, and with it, another metaphor.

Not surprisingly, the paddling metaphor relates the day-to-day challenges a person faces to those one might encounter while navigating a river by canoe. Mostly, it's a "go with the flow" kind of metaphor—a metaphor that sits placidly in the bow on a hot day with its hat pulled across its face and its feet dangling in the water. It's a metaphor that grins uncontrollably as the canoe careens through rapids. It's a metaphor that enjoys getting wet. And the occasional portage? Well, I suppose every life is bound to have a few hiccups from time to time.

I think you can see why the paddling metaphor has great appeal. Doesn't a canoe (like life) follow the river's twists and turns, every bend hiding what you'll encounter next? Doesn't a canoe (like life) drift along, at peace with its surroundings, and then suddenly find itself crashing through whitewater? And doesn't a canoe (like life) sometimes get hung up on rocks—and perhaps, occasionally, empty its contents in the middle of the river? It's in *these* rare instances, of course, when you feel like the river (or your fiancée) is trying to drown you. And it's with this metaphor in mind that Stacey and I embarked on our month-long canoe trip.

*   *   *

Here's a question: what exactly should one say in the event, albeit unlikely, that one finds oneself between a capsized canoe and one's fiancée of two weeks, smashing into boulders and bodysurfing through three-foot standing waves? I'm sure Socrates and other great philosophers must have pondered such questions, though I'm not certain they ever came up with a good answer. Indeed, Socrates might still have chugged the hemlock rather than find out firsthand.

"I'm sorry," I spluttered as we were swept downriver. "I think that was my fault."

"What happened?" asked my soggy sweetheart, spitting water.

"I think the upstream edge of our canoe dipped below one of those waves," I shouted over the roar of the rapids. And now we were inside that industrial washing machine I mentioned, trying to claw our way out.

Fortunately for us, some other canoeists were close at hand. After we had washed out at the end of the rapids, they appeared at our side to pull us out and help us recover our canoe. At least we had carried our gear along the portage trail, so it was safe and dry, waiting for us when we crawled up on shore.

In the end, we pitched camp at the base of those rapids so that we could try "the run" several more times. Of all the rapids along the Missinaibi River, these ones ultimately proved to be our favourites. The portage trail is short and flat, the whitewater is sizable, and there are few serious consequences should you happen to dunk your sweetie in the drink. Except that you might end up doing dishes for the next week.

Stacey and I were ten days into our trip, and we had been through a lot together. We had paddled two hundred and thirty of the roughly seven hundred kilometres on our route, and we'd already had a couple of close calls. On Day Four we had nearly swamped our canoe in the middle of a large lake during a windstorm, and shortly thereafter, we had been bluff charged by a protective mother moose.

The worst of our woes, of course, were the swarms of hungry black flies and mosquitoes, a category of misery unto themselves. Stacey's neck looked like a map of the US eastern seaboard, every red bite mark representing a city or suburb between Massachusetts and Maryland.

But there had been soulful moments, too, like the morning we woke up to find mist swirling across the glassy surface of the lake we had camped beside. The mist's silvery tentacles slithered between several offshore islands as the tangerine-coloured sky breathed life into a new day. We shoved our canoe onto the water, and less than two miles from our campsite became enveloped in the mist as we glided silently past cliffs at Fairy Point, sharing a trajectory with a beaver that was out on morning errands. In the distance we could hear wolves howling, answered, it seemed, by loons a few seconds later. We could feel serenity manifesting on the lake and in our relationship. These are the kinds of experiences that can bond people together for a lifetime.

By Day Eight, an oppressive heat wave had struck, so spending time in the water was actually a welcome antidote. The hot, humid weather was unrelenting, and we spent many lazy hours soaking in the river. A few campsites were even equipped with small waterfalls, which was like having a natural spa in our own backyard.

Another consequence of the heat wave was the dropping of water levels. Rapids became increasingly shallow and bony, and there was usually only one plausible route through the rocky swifts. This meant Stacey would often have to stand up in the bow to scout while we were moving. She did her best to pick the deepest channel, and more often than not she was right. At times I would question her judgment, follow my own instincts, and beach the canoe on some hidden shoal of rocks a few seconds later.

Still, we grew to respect our different ways of doing things and laugh at our own and each other's foibles. This much time in such close quarters can be very intense. Yet we grew closer, we bickered less, and we found new things to share, often things that had been buried under years of memories.

We also developed an efficient routine. Whenever we arrived at a new camp, I would organize and set up the tent while Stacey cooked dinner. She cooked stew and dumplings, pizza, fruit and nut curries, and Mexican fiestas. We ate a lot, laughed a lot, sang songs, and read to each other every night until one of us would drift off to sleep.

*   *   *

Late one afternoon during our third week, Stacey and I approached a large, flat, rectangular rock smack in the middle of the river. It had been another hot day, so on a whim we decided to take a closer look at the rock as a potential campsite. Since we had left the Canadian Shield for the St. James Lowlands, the riverbanks had been getting increasingly brushy and, not surprisingly, infested with large populations of mosquitoes. And I don't care who you are, camping starts to lose its appeal when there are so many mosquitoes that you have to suck up your dinner through a straw that you've poked through the screen in your bug jacket.

It didn't take much to convince us that the rock was a superior campsite. First, its lack of foliage and its strategic position in the middle of the river made it unfit for habitation by mosquitoes. Second, it was completely and utterly unprotected, which meant that if there were even a slight breeze, it would seem magnified tenfold. And where there was wind, we reasoned, there would *definitely* be no mosquitoes. We envisioned laying our sleeping bags across the rock and drifting to sleep under a canopy of stars.

My, how we were wrong.

First of all, nobody had bothered to tell the resident mosquitoes that "our" rock was poor habitat. We swatted our first mozzie just before sunset, and by the time twilight held sway, the little blighters were swarming us.

Determined to stand our ground, we donned our bug jackets and slid deep into our mummy bags, lying on our backs to watch the stars come out. Unfortunately, all we could see were black clouds of mozzies swarming our face nets, and all we could hear was a horrible droning sound reminiscent of the roar a jumbo jet makes while taxiing for takeoff. Even this we were prepared to endure, until we realized that they were biting us through the mesh. For twenty minutes we tried various tactics to stave them off, but nothing seemed to work.

Eventually, we decided to take the only course of action that seemed logical at the time: we would set up our tent on the rock. The good news was that the rock was just wide enough for the tent;

the bad news was that there was nowhere to stake it down.

"The sky is clear and there's no wind," I said. "We should be fine."

Stacey seemed reluctant. "I don't know," she replied.

"Trust me," I reassured her.

We set up the tent, wrestled our way inside, and spent several minutes hunting down and killing all the mosquitoes that had managed to breach our defences, which left us feeling rather smug. "Try getting us now, you little bastards!" I chortled fiendishly.

We stared at the clouds of insects swarming against the far side of the tent screen. Behind them, we could see the first stars appearing in the evening sky.

Around three in the morning, I woke to the faint flutter of wind rustling the tent. I squinted through the screen and found two surprises: no stars and no mosquitoes. Alas, there was no moon either, so I couldn't see anything thing else.

Then there was a sudden flash of light and, a few seconds later, a low guttural rumble, as though God were clearing his throat. Apparently, two weeks of perfect weather were about to break, and we were camped in about the worst place imaginable.

It's in situations like these—when your tent is being flattened by gale-force winds; when rain is soaking you through a tent with no waterproof fly; when lightning is crackling around your ears—that a relationship is put to the acid test. As lightning sliced across the sky, I desperately tried to disassemble our tent while simultaneously scooping up loose articles of clothing before they were blown to Neverland.

It must have been quite the sight: me in my underwear, dancing around on a large rock in the middle of the Missinaibi River. For her part, Stacey flattened herself against the bottom of our tent to prevent it from being airlifted to Quebec.

We stuffed everything into the canoe at odd angles. Then, because we couldn't find either of the headlamps, Stacey gripped a flashlight in her teeth while I steered our overburdened steed through the maelstrom. We bounced off a few rocks, surfed backwards for a while, did a little canoe pirouette, and somehow, quite miraculously, we made it to shore without capsizing.

The riverbank was rocky and pitched at an odd angle, but at least there was some shelter. As the wind and rain continued to pelt in sideways, we pitched our tent behind some bushes on sloping, muddy ground.

After what seemed a short eternity, we climbed into the wet tent to wait out the rest of the storm. We were tired. Our nerves were frazzled. Everything was soaked. It had been my idea to camp on the rock, and I couldn't blame Stacey if she were mad at me.

As we inventoried our belongings, I half-expected an "I told you so" lecture, or at least a disgruntled disposition. When I turned to face my sweetheart, however, I found a look not of anger, but of tenderness. She was smiling at me.

"I love you," she said.

"I love you too."

Then we climbed into our soppy sleeping bags, snuggled up together, and fell asleep to the sound of a storm beating hard against our home away from home. It was Day Twenty of eighteen thousand, two hundred and sixty-seven, and there was no place I would rather have been.

Epilogue

The trip ended when we loaded our canoe onto a special railcar at the Moosonee train station, twenty kilometres south of James Bay. Stacey and I had spent the last two nights camped under a grove of cottonwood trees on Charles Island, reflecting on our epic journey. We had learned a lot about canoe tripping and about each other.

I won't go into details, but we learned that Stacey is usually right, and that I need to work on my whitewater skills. But I can tell you another thing. If you happen to get engaged, plan a long-distance canoe trip *before* getting hitched. Can you think of a better opportunity to dunk your life partner without being under contract?

Matt Jackson is the president of Summit Studios and author of the award-winning book, The Canada Chronicles: A Four-Year Hitchhiking Odyssey. *Stacey Fitzsimmons is a PhD student studying cross-cultural management at Simon Fraser University in Vancouver. She acknowledges that sometimes, every so often, Matt is right.*

Moose Masseuse

Can a group of skiers save Bullwinkle from an unpleasant demise?

By Hazel Booth

For many years I worked as a nurse in Ottawa, Canada's bustling capital. It's a beautiful city, but I also wanted to experience nursing in other parts of the country. The word was out in the northern nursing community: the Yukon was a great place. So I packed up and moved to the "great white north" in Canada's Yukon Territory. It didn't take me long to feel at home there, with the fresh air and boundless spaces.

In 2004, for the first time ever, I was not working on Christmas day or returning to Ontario to visit family. I decided to do something special—celebrate the holidays by skiing into a backcountry cabin for several days with Yukon friends Sean and Matt.

My brother Grant, intrigued by my stories of Canada's North, had recently followed me to the Yukon and we asked him to join us. The cabin where we planned to stay was located near Haines Pass, a stunning area along the edge of Kluane National Park. The region has mountains and lakes galore—a true winter wonderland.

On Christmas Day, the four of us crammed into Sean's little truck. Gear was jammed into every conceivable nook in the back, and our snowboards and skis were lashed to the top. We left Whitehorse late that afternoon, just as it was starting to get dark. Warm weather had made the roads greasy, and a few kilometres down the road we stopped to help some travellers whose car had slid off the road and landed on its roof.

We planned to get gas in Haines Junction, but because it was Christmas Day, every gas station was closed. We decided that driving to the cabin without a full tank of gas would be foolish; running out of gas on the Haines Road would not be a good thing in minus-thirty-degree weather.

Matt thought we should drive as far as Kathleen Lake and stay at a day-use cabin that had a wood-burning stove. In the morning, we would double back to Haines Junction to get gas.

We arrived at the cabin and immediately settled in. Soon the wood stove was roaring and we started to make Christmas dinner. No turkey for the likes of us—we had brought caribou, sheep, and buffalo meat, and made a scrumptious fondue.

Feeling stuffed, we decided to go for a walk after dinner. As we approached the lake, though, we heard strange gurgling and groaning noises. The lake seemed unsettled—like it had indigestion. I had never heard anything like it.

On Boxing Day, Sean drove the truck back to Haines Junction to gas up while the rest of us made breakfast. Matt and Sean had heard of some ice climbing at the far end of Kathleen Lake and were interested in trying to find it, so we decided to spend the day there and ski into the backcountry cabin early in the evening.

The previous year, members of the local community had made some snowshoes and warm mukluks for me. I was anxious to try them out. Grant had some modern snowshoes, and Matt and Sean decided to ski and pull the ice climbing gear in toboggans behind them.

About an hour across the lake, Grant called to me, "Hey, Hazel, are moose supposed to be in the water at this time of year?" He pointed to what he thought was a moose. It looked like a rock to me … until it moved. As we approached, we quickly realized the moose had fallen through the ice.

Cautiously, we approached the moose; we weren't sure if it would charge us, but it quickly became apparent that we were in no danger. The moose was stuck in the ice, shivering uncontrollably; the poor beast must have been exhausted. A horseshoe-shaped path through the ice indicated where the moose had struggled to get out, with no success. Clearly, he wasn't much of an ice dancer. Covered in ice, he tinkled like a Christmas tree whenever he moved. We realized sadly that he was helpless and would eventually die.

We tried yelling at the moose to scare him out of the water. Nothing. We chipped away at some of the ice around him with ski poles. He still didn't budge. "Maybe he just needs some energy," I said hopefully. I grabbed my curried tuna wrap from the sled and Matt tried feeding it to him, but he wouldn't eat it. Curried tuna obviously wasn't his thing, nor were a bagel and some trail mix.

Our next strategy involved the use of rope that Matt and Sean had brought for ice climbing. We tied it loosely around the moose's neck and pulled. My heart despaired as our friend—I dubbed him

Morris—lost his leverage and sank deeper into the water. He was going under. We had made the situation worse, and I was starting to feel nauseous.

Then Matt and Sean had an idea. Matt and I kept tension on the rope to keep Morris's head afloat while Sean set up a crevasse pulley system that would give us a huge mechanical advantage. Sean hurriedly rigged the pulleys using some ice screws, while Matt and I worked to loop the rope around poor Morris. It was a bit of a challenge to get the rope through the frigid water and under his shoulders, but we eventually managed to do it.

Meanwhile, Grant put Morris in a headlock. As Grant would later say, he was "cheek to cheek and eye to eye with the moose." Morris pushed against Grant and they both used the side of the ice as leverage while Matt, Sean, and I pulled on the rope.

Slowly we pulled Morris out of the water, about a metre from where he'd fallen through the ice. "WE DID IT!" I shouted gleefully. Morris was finally out of the water. But what were we going to do now? The poor moose was lying helplessly on the ice, shivering.

Thankfully, it all came together. We draped Matt's tarp over Morris and built a shelter to shield him from the wind and blowing snow. Then we gathered firewood and lit a small fire inside the shelter to keep him warm. We even had warm water in some Nalgene bottles, so we pried open his mouth and poured it down his throat. We pulled ice off his fur. We massaged the muscles in his hind legs, and in fact, stopped just short of giving him a manicure and pedicure. Would we henceforth be known as Canada's first moose masseuses?

Careful as we were while working, Matt fell through the ice up to his waist, quickly hauling himself out. I was next to fall in as I carried a big boulder to the snow fort. It must have been a bit too heavy, as my right foot slipped through the ice up to my knee. Then Sean's foot slipped through. We teased Grant that he would be next.

Matt, Sean, and Grant successfully pull Morris out of the icy crevasse. Whenever Morris moved, he sounded like a tinkling Christmas tree.

Morris lay there, turning his head occasionally to get a better look at us, looking much like a dog cozied up to a fireplace. It was all too bizarre. Often we forgot he was even there, until one of us would suddenly giggle and say, "Um, is that a moose right there?"

Around six or seven p.m., Morris started to perk up, paying more attention to his surroundings and even drooling a bit. At one point he tried to stand up, but fell down again, his butt almost landing on the fire. Perhaps Morris just wanted to warm his behind!

At this point, we were starting to get cold and hungry ourselves. We didn't know what else to do for Morris, so we put on our snowshoes and skis and headed back toward camp in the dark. By the time we arrived, we were all too tired to search for the backcountry cabin, so we decided to stay put for another night. Besides, we wanted to check on our new friend in the morning.

It was very early when we set out across the lake to find Morris. We skied silently, anxious about what we would find. Would he be there? Would he have fallen through the ice again? Would he be alive? As we approached the scene of yesterday's rescue, we couldn't hear or see any sign of a moose. We peered into the snow shelter and found it empty. He was gone! One of the walls had been knocked over and his tracks led off into the distance. Only remnants of the fire and two untouched bagels were left behind.

We were ecstatic. I threw my arms around Sean, who happened to be standing next to me, while Grant and Matt started following his tracks. Grant found him a couple of hundred metres away, in the first bush that offered shelter. When he saw us, he promptly fell down, but we were pleased to see he'd been eating some willows and depositing moose droppings across the snow. Morris was definitely looking stronger.

We continued across the lake, but never did find the ice climb. On our way back in the late afternoon, we stopped to check on Morris. This time he was standing, and looking a bit more wary about us being so close. Interestingly, he would not let Matt, Sean, or me get closer than a few metres. Grant, however, who had been "cheek to cheek and eye to eye" with him, put his hand out and he responded. Slowly, he brought his nose down and touched Grant's hand, as if to say, "Hey, man, thanks for helping me out of a jam."

We stood around and chatted to Morris for a few minutes. We told him not to worry, that falling through the ice could happen to anyone. We also warned him that he was going to need a bit of a makeover. His friends would no doubt be suspicious when they saw him, considering that he still sounded like a Christmas tree whenever he moved. We also warned him to run the other way if he saw people dressed in green, yellow, and black.

I think all of us half-expected Morris to follow us back to camp. I caught myself looking over my shoulder every few minutes, but of course, he didn't.

The lake was quiet that night—no gurgling or groaning. Perhaps the indigestion had passed. With only one night of our holidays remaining, we set out to look for the backcountry cabin. But the road was sheet ice and the wind was blowing hard, so we stayed at another tiny roadside cabin. When we awoke in the morning, about two feet of fresh snow had blown through a crack in the door. It had been a cold night.

The drive back to Whitehorse proved to be another adventure worthy of Christmas in the Yukon. We plowed through huge snowdrifts and fought against poor visibility, gale-force winds, and icy roads. Not that the conditions really bothered us. We had saved Morris's life, and it would be some time before the peaceful glow of helping our new friend vanished from our thoughts.

Hazel, Matt, and Sean still live, work, and play in the Yukon Territory. They've returned to Kluane National Park several times, but haven't seen Morris since his rescue. Grant resides in Ottawa, Ontario.

The Endless Climb

Alpinist John Lauchlan thrived on the dangers that led to his death on Cirrus Mountain. A friend reflects on the spiritual lessons of a life spent risking it all.

By Jim Scott

I t's a scene that has played itself out in my mind so many times that it now seems like my own experience, as though it were me who had just scaled the ice column and now traversed the steep snow patch to the next pillar, ice tools clutched in each hand, cramponed boots punching a serrated line across the snow. The mind focuses on the hundreds of metres of vertical ice still to ascend. Then … muscles spring taut as the snow slab tears free. Legs and arms flail in the first frantic thrust for a firm hold. Tools and crampon points stab desperately into the dense white air. The body tumbles, bounces, twists as the avalanche builds, sluicing clean the short, sloping ledge.

Then nothing. Free fall. An arcing plummet in a white void, ice tools trailing on their tethers like futile anchors. The impact on the rocks …

No. I never make it to the rocks. Every time I replay this fall, I struggle to get into the climber's mind just after the ice tools and the crampons fail him, after he leaves the rock and ice for what he immediately knows to be the last time. But while I can be swept vicariously off the ledge in an avalanche, I cannot simulate his consciousness during free fall. No matter how many times I have started across the snow patch, I have never been able to put myself into the mind of someone who, after years of self-imperilment, is about to die.

As a fellow climber, I had been close to John Lauchlan's mind, but never close enough to determine the role he assigned to death, a role more acutely defined and more unflinchingly accepted than is possible in those who could never climb unroped up hundreds of metres of vertical ice. Whether this definition is a cause or a consequence of such climbing is impossible to say, but it was clearly a fundamental ordering principle for his life, like a seed crystal that brings everything around it into a pattern at once coherent and beautiful. A pattern in which big abstractions such as Meaning and Purpose have settled neatly into place.

Each venture of mine across the snow patch is a renewed attempt to find this pattern that must preclude fear, must make a death plummet something other than a termination point. Having learned from John about the isolation of the self within and by means of the wilderness, I feel certain that the fall would assume the place he had prepared for it. His 1982 plunge alongside the ice columns of Cirrus Mountain in Alberta would have been the final adjustment of a counterweight, the concluding brush stroke that balances and completes the picture.

John Lauchlan taught me how to climb. He urged me up rocks and glaciers and frozen waterfalls, showing me how to set up anchor systems and to move with efficiency across a sequence of scant holds. Before meeting him in 1979, I had taken a basic climbing course—but only because I was terrified of heights and wanted to know how to handle ropes if the need arose on any of my backpacking trips.

The course, however, took me like a drug, animating me into an intensity of consciousness that was both fascinating and abominating. Perched on a half-centimetre spur of rock, secured from above by a rope, I was exhilarated. No vertigo. And with no fear of falling, I found I could move with impunity over the rock wall, pitting my strength and balance against the thin nubs and cracks coded into the mountain's face. Well, not total impunity. A mistake would result in a scraping slide of a few metres, although I was surprised to discover that I virtually never slipped, almost as if the rope extending up from my waist acted like a talisman that warded off gravity.

But there were times when, moving spread-eagled up through a section of thin holds and arriving at the security of a half-metre-wide ledge, I wondered about the talisman. What if the rope wasn't there? What would be my state of mind if there was just me and the austere face of the mountain, so indifferent to my mote-like presence?

That's what led me to John Lauchlan.

John taught climbing courses throughout the late 1970s and into the early 1980s at the Yamnuska Mountain School near Canmore, Alberta. The son of a former University of Calgary chaplain, he had grown to regard orthodoxy as the mind's most potent enemy; he continually strove to liberate himself from reliance on anything external to his own capacities. I always saw in him the same aspirations that had animated the Romantic poets: the spiritual odyssey, the quest for realization of all that lies latent in the universe of the individual mind, the spurning of security as a precondition for expansion of consciousness.

I once quoted to him a few of William Blake's Proverbs of Hell from *The Marriage of Heaven and Hell*: "No bird soars too high if he soars with his own wings"; "You never know what is enough unless you know what is more than enough"; "Thus men forget that all deities reside in the human breast." He nodded enthusiastically, saying, "Exactly, exactly."

Climbing was more than a sport to him, it was a medium through which he engaged with life more intimately than he ever could otherwise. And each climb was more than a test of his skills—it was an extension of the boundaries of the known into the unknown, however incommunicable this knowledge necessarily was. Each climb opened a little wider his doors of perception.

I spent a night with him back in 1980, bivouacked just below the summit face of Alberta's Mount Victoria, getting the reverse view to the one on countless postcard photos of Lake Louise. We had scaled Mount Aberdeen the previous day and had then made our way up through the glaciers that inch down Victoria's flanks.

The night air was mild, and without an overnight freeze, the remaining two hundred and forty metres of the face would become a shooting gallery of rocks released by the ever-exfoliating limestone. Our discussion of the risk awaiting us in the morning led to the principle that informs all mountaineering: the value of peril, the philosophy of self-jeopardy.

Wending our way up that day through an extensive matrix of crevasses, we had been confronted at one point by a long, bottomless crevasse bridged only by a thin patch of snow that had not yet been melted by the summer sun. John asked whether I wanted to go for it, although we both knew that despite being roped together, crevasse rescue in such situations can be impossible. I said yes, and he anchored the rope while I crossed, and then I did the same for him.

That night, John asked me what I felt as I stepped onto the bridge. I said that I felt as though someone had rasped sandpaper across all the nerve endings in my body. My neck hair was pricked erect, and my muscles almost ached in anticipation of the reflex moves I would make the instant I felt the bridge buckling. I could give a microsecond-by-microsecond description of the motions my body went through during the four-second crossing.

He said, "Right." For him, intensity was incompatible with security. And the extent to which one experiences intensity was, by his standards, a measure of the value of life.

That night on Victoria, I had tried to find out what *his* experience had been on the thin snow bridge—indeed, what had driven him to spend virtually all his time pitting himself against the wilderness at its most redoubtable. He mentioned what had become an aphorism among mountaineers: "You don't conquer a mountain, you use a mountain to conquer something within yourself." But the most fascinating aspect, John said, is that the conquering never ends.

Each climb just registers in the mind in different ways, perhaps because the mind takes on a different composition as a result of each climb. The reaching for, not the grasping of, is valuable.

John was always puzzled by the people who asked him what it was like when he stood atop Mount Logan in the Yukon, Canada's highest peak, after leading a team up its previously unclimbed southwest buttress. "If my goal had simply been to stand on top of the buttress, imagine how disappointed I'd be, being twenty-four years old and having met my goal."

He loved to tell the story of the time he and another climber had done a multi-day ascent up the north face of Alberta's Mount Temple. Like many peaks in the Rockies, Temple has a precipitous face on one side with a hiking trail up the other, more gently sloping side. When John pulled himself over the lip of the thirty-metre icecap that crowns the north face, he found himself a few metres away from a couple of hikers who had walked to the summit. Astounded at seeing John, one of them asked where he had come from, so he briefly described the climb and the hanging bivouac. The hiker almost laughed in amazement and, pointing to the south slope of the mountain, said, "Oh, for cripe's sake, there's a trail just over here!"

I remember clarifying for John my understanding of existential philosophy, at least as I saw it surfacing in poems and novels. I mentioned the recoil-from-the-void image, the revulsion that some of Sartre's and Hemingway's characters undergo when they somehow see life stripped of all its distracting surfaces, thereby revealing the meaningless morass that is the fundamental condition of life.

He had already *lived* such an experience on the Mount Logan climb. An attempt the previous year had been aborted, so when he and his team embarked on their climb the second time, they felt they could move rapidly through the previously climbed section regardless of weather. John was leading a particularly steep pitch in dense, low-lying cloud, but he knew that at the top there was a broad ledge on which they could safely station themselves. When he arrived there, visibility was almost nil, but he was content in the awareness that he was in a solid and secure place.

However, as often happens when high alpine reaches are shrouded in swirling cloud, the fog suddenly dissipated, momentarily giving him a clear survey of his situation. Only later did he learn of the previous winter's earthquake whose epicentre had been in the Logan area. What he saw when the fog parted was nothing—the entire ledge had calved off, leaving only the small fragment on which he was casually standing. The solidity was a delusion; the contentment was derived from a failure (perhaps even a wilful failure) to see other than what we expect or desire to see. The void was real; security, illusory. And John was on the edge of the abyss, and not balking at what he saw. In fact, rather than fleeing this reality, John revelled in it.

But John didn't ridicule those who couldn't cope with jeopardy. On the second day of my advanced mountaineering course with him, I had camped with three others below the ice couloir that runs up the face of Mount Narao near Lake Louise. John's watch alarm went off at four a.m., and he called out to wake us up. A voice in the dark beside me said: "I can't do it. I've been awake all night thinking about this, and I just can't do it."

After a pause, John said: "Right. It's good you understand. We'll walk back to the car with you." And we did.

The last time I saw John alive was in Kathmandu. I'd taken a year off work to travel in Asia and Africa, and he was going to push a new route up Mount Gangapurna, so I had agreed to meet him in Nepal and help his team pack gear into their base camp. However, the standard Nepalese bureaucratic burlesque held up his departure for three weeks, so as he suggested, I did the long trek east into the Everest Base Camp region. After returning, I tried to catch up with his team as they and their porters slowly worked their way west toward base camp in the Annapurna Sanctuary.

On my way in I met Mary, his wife of a few months, who was on her way out. She told me of the rigours on the team's hike and said I might catch John at the base camp if I hurried. I pushed on as fast as I could but had to quit when I got bogged down in deep, wet snow inside the Sanctuary, the same snow that had caused the porters to retreat.

John and three other climbers were forced to ferry all their supplies up to the base camp; then, halfway up the south face, two of the three climbers had to turn back because of altitude sickness. The other climber, James Blench, also felt like retreating, but "fuelled more by John's motivation than my own resources," he accompanied John for three more days until they stood alone on the summit—the first new route Canadian climbers had ever established on a Himalayan peak.

I stayed in the Sanctuary for a day. Occasionally I tried to pick out motes moving up the face of Gangapurna, but I spent most of the day seated on a moraine, keenly aware that my life had fallen wonderfully into balance, that I could ask no more of myself than what I was. I could never climb a Himalayan face, and I would never live as precariously or as intensely as John did— but I had found my limits. And as I sat alone in the Sanctuary, breathing the cold, thin air and gazing up at the peaks looming thousands of metres above me, I realized John had led me there. Or rather, he had started me in this direction so that over time, I could bring myself into this perfect insularity, this sanctuary inviolable by doubt.

John, however, moved much deeper into the spiritual sanctuary, leaving me to wonder what lay in there, what definitions and patterns come into focus as one moves far beyond the murk of security. He started soloing—climbing alone on faces, without anchors or ropes or belay systems to catch him in the event of a slip. He never spoke of this as though climbers on ropes were in any way inferior or cowardly. For him, it was the move into total self-reliance, where judgment of or by others was immaterial. The necessity of being impeccably right made him impeccably alive.

For years, John had been impeccably right while doing unheard-of solo climbs. He made the first solo ascent of the three-hundred-metre ice wall at Takakkaw Falls in British Columbia's Yoho National Park, and at a 1980 mountaineers' convention in the Alps near Chamonix, France, he soloed the Gaborou Couloir while the world's best climbers watched in disbelief.

As one of Canada's premier alpinists, John was to be a major figure in the Canadian Mount Everest expedition in 1982. He realized that in every climb, the cost of one misplaced crampon or one misjudgment of ice thickness was death. Many of his climbing friends had died in falls, and he had had close brushes with death.

He once tripped while descending after a climb, and only because his rope snagged a rock outcropping did he avoid a six-hundred-metre slide into a crevasse. Once, while he and I were camped miserably in bad weather on a small ledge, he described an aborted winter climb during which he and his partner were forced to retreat into a shallow cave scooped into a steep slope while spindrift avalanches continually whirled past them. Every ten minutes they monitored each other's condition by asking, "Dead yet?"

Like most climbers I've known, John never discussed death as a metaphysical state or as a cause of others' bereavement. Death is simply the collateral you offer in order to attain a quickened sense of life. Perhaps it is this cavalier attitude that keeps many climbers single. However, a few, such as John, find a kindred spirit who recognizes and even extols the value of climbing. Mary, herself a climber, no doubt knew that she and John had to pursue their separate challenges. For their love to be a positive force it had to accommodate, not stifle, what each was extracting from life.

But for me, this conflict of values resolved itself differently three years after my Himalayan trip, by which time I had a wife and two toddlers. I was facing a series of risky moves across a patch of steep glacial ice. The weather was bad, the ice was frangible, a crevasse gaped open below me—but my focus wasn't on the climb. With unprecedented clarity, I visualized the consequences of my death, the devastating impact on my family if I never returned home. The climb itself soon had to be aborted, but I knew then that for me, the edge was gone, or rather, that one chapter in my life was over and that a new one with different gratifications was beginning.

Still, I struggle to discover what crossed John's mind when, for all his impeccable rightness, all his convictions about the value of jeopardy, he plummeted amid an avalanche toward the rocks at the base of Cirrus Mountain. Had he successfully brought himself into the state of mind where life's value lay purely in intensity rather than in duration? Where what happens within any one second is more significant than how many seconds are strung together in sequence? Is mortality a different state for minds inside the sanctuary? Yes. He had led me to discover that.

It is this conviction that John, at the age of twenty-seven, had managed through intensity to detach his consciousness from the passage of time that leads me to start again across the snow patch, to try to enter a mind fallen free from conventional measures of time and value. I realize I will never venture as far as John did, but I find solace in the belief that his fall from Cirrus was of little consequence because of the life that preceded it.

By moving into a state of consummate self-reliance, John could never arrive at an end point. He has not yet hit the rocks.

Jim Scott, now an instructor at Red Deer College, learned mountaineering from John Lauchlan thirty years ago. He still spends time in the mountains, where the spirit of his mentor continues to inspire him.

Do you have a Great Story?

If you enjoyed this collection of stories and feel you have an outrageous, funny, heartwarming or inspirational tale that you would like to share, we would love to hear from you. Our only rules are that your story has some unusual, illuminating or humorous twist to it, that it's true and that it has something to do with spending time in the Great Outdoors.

We are already working on a follow-up to *Mugged by a Moose* and we can accept either story outlines or pieces that have already been written. You don't have to be a professional writer. We look forward to hearing from anybody that has a great yarn to spin.

To obtain more detailed submission guidelines, please visit Summit Studios on our web site at:

www.summitstudios.biz

Please submit stories or story outlines by e-mail, fax or snail mail to:

SUMMIT STUDIOS
#105, 2572 Birch St.
Vancouver, BC V6H 2T4
Fax: (778) 371-8561
E-mail: submissions@summitstudios.biz

We look forward to hearing from you.

Acknowledgements

A very special thanks to my fianceé, Stacey, who shares my passion for travel and the outdoors. Her unconditional support and her belief in my dream to found a publishing company have made this book possible.

Thanks to my family and friends who have offered ideas, support, and critical feedback as this book has taken shape.

Thanks to Marion Harrison and Yvonne Jeffery for help with the editing, and to Kirk Seton for a great book design.

And finally, thanks to the many outdoor lovers who have contributed their stories to this book. Your willingness to share means that all of us are a little richer.

About Matt Jackson

A graduate of Wilfrid Laurier's Business Administration program, Matt Jackson was lured away from the corporate world by the thrill of adventure journalism while still a university student. He is now an author, photojournalist and professional speaker, and is the president of Summit Studios, a publishing company specializing in books about travel and the outdoors.

Matt's first book, *The Canada Chronicles: A Four-Year Hitchhiking Odyssey*, won the IPPY award for best North American travel memoir in 2004. His work has also been featured in more than two dozen popular magazines including *Equinox*, *Explore*, *Photo Life*, *Canadian Geographic* and *BBC Wildlife*. He currently lives in Vancouver.